New Year's Resolutions

Mastering the Art of Meaningful Change

(The Guide to Getting It Right Why Many New Year Resolutions Fail Within 30 Days)

Peter Hanson

Published By **John Kembrey**

Peter Hanson

All Rights Reserved

New Year's Resolutions: Mastering the Art of Meaningful Change (The Guide to Getting It Right Why Many New Year Resolutions Fail Within 30 Days)

ISBN 978-1-7781960-6-5

No part of this guidebook shall be reproduced in any form without permission in writing from the publisher except in the case of brief quotations embodied in critical articles or reviews.

Legal & Disclaimer

The information contained in this book is not designed to replace or take the place of any form of medicine or professional medical advice. The information in this book has been provided for educational & entertainment purposes only.

The information contained in this book has been compiled from sources deemed reliable, and it is accurate to the best of the Author's knowledge; however, the Author cannot guarantee its accuracy and validity and cannot be held liable for any errors or omissions. Changes are periodically made to this book. You must consult your doctor or get professional medical advice before using any of the suggested remedies, techniques, or information in this book.

Upon using the information contained in this book, you agree to hold harmless the Author from and against any damages, costs, and expenses, including any legal fees potentially resulting from the application of any of the information provided by this guide. This disclaimer applies to any damages or injury caused by the use and application, whether directly or indirectly, of any advice or information presented, whether for breach of contract, tort, negligence, personal injury, criminal intent, or under any other cause of action.

You agree to accept all risks of using the information presented inside this book. You need to consult a professional medical practitioner in order to ensure you are both able and healthy enough to participate in this program.

Table Of Contents

Chapter 1: Resolution 1

Chapter 2: Setting Meaningful Goals 11

Chapter 3: Skill Development.................. 29

Chapter 4: Personal Growth.................... 41

Chapter 5: Time Management 63

Chapter 6: Overcoming Challenges And Relapses... 80

Chapter 7: When And Why?.................... 91

Chapter 8: The Personal Change Process 99

Chapter 9: How To Make New Year's Resolutions 103

Chapter 10: Resolution Ideas For 2024 121

Chapter 11: Compassion And Self Kindness 151

Chapter 12: Mindfulness Practices........ 160

Chapter 13: Building A Positive Mindset 177

Chapter 1: Resolution

WHAT ARE NEW YEAR RESOLUTIONS?

New Year's resolutions are individualized commitments or ensures humans make to themselves to perform particular dreams or beautify one-of-a-type sides of their lives on the begin of a present day twelve months. These desires can range drastically and deal with an entire lot of topics, inclusive of relationships, hobby improvement, personal growth, health, and fitness. The motive of putting desires for private improvement and self-development is to capitalize at the possibility for a clean begin that a modern-day 3 hundred and sixty five days gives. New Year's resolutions are a commonplace custom; however whether they'll be a fulfillment or now not regularly is based on how devoted, prepared, and pushed the individual is to art work closer to their desires all year lengthy.

Importance of Self-Improvement Resolutions

Self-development desires are very critical for numerous motives:

Personal Development

The way of non-stop self-development, self-discovery, and personal improvement is called non-public increase. It consists of creating a deliberate attempt to amplify one's studies, understanding base, and stage of highbrow, emotional, and religious improvement. A person's non-public development consists of numerous aspects of their life, together with:

Self-Awareness: Being aware about 1's virtues, vices, values, and beliefs.

Education And Learning: Increasing one's records base and selecting up new skills through exceptional schooling, independent have a study, or hands-on schooling.

Emotional Intelligence: Mastering the functionality to apprehend, alter, and correctly interact with others.

Self-Esteem And Confidence: Developing a excellent experience of oneself and self-notion in a single's abilities.

Interpersonal talents: strengthening bonds, exchanges of mind, and potential for empathy.

Setting And Achieving Goals: Establishing and undertaking every expert and private targets.

Adaptability: embracing traumatic conditions, being bendy, and choosing up commands from failures.

Physical And Mental Well-Being: emphasizing stress bargain, mental well-being, and physical health.

Spirituality And Mindfulness: Investigating one's non secular beliefs and appealing in mindfulness physical video games to gather inner harmony and tranquility.

A lifetime journey in the direction of self-achievement, more high-quality excellent of life, and a more profound comprehension of oneself and the world spherical you are all viable effects of personal growth. It frequently includes goal-setting, introspection, and a willpower to ongoing progress.

Building Skills

They provide the hazard to pick out out up new abilties, statistics, and talents which could enhance one's relationships, profession, and considerable properly-being. Developing competencies is a critical thing of resolving self-improvement for numerous motives:

Personal Growth: Accomplishment and a experience of accomplishment can cease end result from mastering new competencies or refining modern-day-day ones. It gives you the danger to push yourself and studies new topics.

Career Advancement: Learning new abilties can enhance your credentials and boom your marketability. Better task opportunities and higher profits ability may additionally prevent end result from it.

Enhanced Confidence: Mastering a records allow you to sense extra confident and right about yourself. Reaching your capability-improvement goals can also make you revel in powerful.

Adaptability: Possessing a severa capability set permits you be extra bendy in a worldwide that is changing all the time. It helps you to exchange course and attain achievement in unique contexts or fields.

Lifelong Learning: Developing one's potential set encourages lifelong studying. It keeps intellectual stimulation and activity, which is right for cognitive feature.

Personal Fulfillment: You may enjoy happy and fulfilled when you pursue pursuits and passions that in form your capabilities.

Problem Solving: Critical wondering and hassle-fixing are common components of expertise improvement, and they will let you grow to be extra adept at dealing with barriers in masses of spheres of lifestyles.

Enhanced Self-Belief

Reaching self-development dreams can provide humans more self assurance and self-esteem, permitting them to tackle probabilities and demanding conditions. Among the not unusual goals of self-improvement resolutions is superior self warranty. Here's how targeting growing your self-guarantee may be a useful part of developing your self:

Self-Esteem Boost: Developing your self-warranty will assist you experience higher approximately your self. You're greater inclined to pursue your objectives and method boundaries with optimism if you have self belief in your capabilities and fee.

Improved Communication: Having greater self perception often effects in advanced communication talents. You're more likely to speak your mind and opinions really and concisely, which could beautify connections on a personal and expert degree.

Taking Calculated Risks: Being confident could probable encourage you to take calculated possibilities that might boom your profession and private development. It assist you to in stepping beyond your consolation area and taking benefit of chances that you might not have in any other case had.

Resilience: Having self-guarantee has a tendency to boom resilience. You're greater able to overcoming setbacks and disappointments due to the reality you note them as possibilities for personal development as opposed to insurmountable barriers.

Career Advancement: Success within the workplace is often correlated with confidence. It can result in advanced standard overall performance in interviews, greater fruitful networking, and the functionality to mentor and uplift others within the place of job.

Personal Relationships: You will have more healthful relationships on your private life with the aid of the use of using having greater self guarantee in your self. Setting limits and efficiently talking your necessities and desires will boom the probability of mutual recognize and progressed know-how.

Contentment and Well-Being: Generally speaking, contentment and properly-being are better in folks who possess self notion. You're much more likely to take part in fun sports, make and meet private dreams, and revel in a feel of success.

You can exercise public talking, make extraordinary self-affirmations, set and gain minor dreams, are looking for for mentorship or counseling, and constantly push yourself to transport outside your comfort quarter as self-improvement resolutions to paintings on boosting yourself perception. These efforts have the functionality to make you a extra self-assured and succesful man or woman in the end.

Well-Being And Health

Health and properly-being-related resolutions can result in a better life-style, lower danger of numerous health troubles, and an greater ideal top notch of existence. It is crucial to prioritize health and well-being as a self-improvement purpose. One of the precept components of private improvement is the subsequent:

Physical Health: Putting your health first let you live an extended life, be extra bodily in shape, and function a lower chance of developing persistent ailments. It gives you more power and power to stay a better pleasant of life.

Emotional Health: It's surely as critical to look after your emotional fitness. You might also moreover furthermore contend with pressure, tension, and despair and construct emotional resilience by using the usage of enhancing yourself in this location.

Increased Productivity: You're much more likely to be targeted and inexperienced at the same time as you are in suitable bodily and intellectual health. You can whole tasks speedy, which improves both your non-public and expert achievement.

Quality of Life: Improving one's fashionable health and properly-being can bring about a better remarkable of existence. You can spend time with loved ones, partake on your favorite activities, and completely encompass life.

Self-Care: Making health and properly-being a priority often includes self-care strategies that help in recharging and reducing burnout. This can comprise practices like everyday workout, mindfulness, getting sufficient sleep, and retaining a wholesome food plan.

Chapter 2: Setting Meaningful Goals
CHOOSING THE RIGHT RESOLUTIONS

Making the right New Year's resolutions is an vital first step for your quest for non-public improvement. Your targets, goals, and personal development can be fashioned via manner of way of the resolutions you area in the path of the twelve months. Selecting the correct resolutions is a excessive desire, despite the fact that. Ensuring your resolutions are relevant, workable, and ordinary together along with your priorities and values takes careful concept and training.

How to make the awesome resolutions for the modern day 365 days

Introspection

Think about your existence, your values, and the areas you want to enhance in advance than making any resolutions. Think about your lengthy-time period desires, areas of strength, and weaknesses. Which areas of your existence are most in want of change?

Making huge resolutions begins with self-mirrored image.

Achievable And Realism

A conventional mistake made even as making resolutions is to aim too excessive or to be excessively bold. It's important to push your self, but your goals want to furthermore be available and less high-priced. Establishing unreachable goals ought to make you revel in annoyed and disenchanted, which can also force you to give up in your resolutions.

Specific And Quantifiable

Try to be as specific and quantifiable as you may at the side of your resolutions. Set extra particular goals, like "workout for 30 minutes, 3 times a week," in region of a fashionable one like "get in shape." This clarity permits you to reveal your development and keep responsibility.

Set Priorities

You might not be able to deal with every detail of your life proper away. Sort your resolutions into precedence lists in keeping with what topics most to you at this thing to your lifestyles. You'll be greater successful if you recognition on a small variety of crucial objectives.

Examine the Long-Term Effects

Consider how your goals for the present day day yr in shape together together with your prolonged-time period desires and beliefs. Do they assist your selected pleasure and nicely-being? The maximum great resolutions are those who yield lengthy-term benefits.

Break It Down

If you have a huge resolution, divide it up into smaller, more workable responsibilities. This lessens the overwhelming feeling and permits you to renowned small victories alongside the road.

Responsibility And Assistance

Tell a member of the family or close pal whom you bear in mind approximately your resolutions at the manner to preserve you accountable. To keep yourself heading within the right course, reflect onconsideration on becoming a member of a assist organization or finding a resolve friend.

Flexibility

Circumstances ought to probable alternate and lifestyles may be unpredictable. Instead of giving up on your resolutions surely while problems emerge, be willing to modify them as important.

Monitor Your Development

To degree your development, make use of a aim-monitoring device or hold a pocket ebook. Evaluate your normal performance often and trade as wanted.

Show Yourself Some Love

Recall that obstacles are a regular part of the technique. Be moderate with your self in case you make mistakes along the street. Turn setbacks into coaching moments and idea to hold going.

SMART Goals: Specific, Measurable, Achievable, Relevant, Time-Bound: New Year's Resolutions

The SMART dreams framework is a useful device to help you with motive-putting in phrases of New Year's resolutions. Using those tips will help you're making easy, viable resolutions that have a higher threat of being achieved.

1. Specific

Your desires need to be specific and smooth to understand. Make your aim specific, like "workout for half of-hour, 3 times according to week," in region of aiming for some issue popular like "get in shape." A more specific selection can be much less difficult to realise and strive within the path of.

2. Measurable

The ability to display your improvement is a critical issue of a success resolves. Ensure that your targets can be measured. If your aim is to study greater, for example, installation a purpose like "take a look at 20 pages a day" or "quit 20 books this year." You can speedy decide how nicely you're doing in this method.

three. Achievable

Your goals ought to be to be had and much less pricey. Although it's far exquisite to push your self, aiming for matters which might be past your reach must motive disappointment or perhaps failure. When making resolutions, keep in mind your talents, sources, and modern-day state of affairs.

four. Relevant

Your dreams for the new three hundred and sixty five days need to align along facet your values, way of lifestyles, and extended-time period desires. They need to be critical to you and everyday alongside facet your popular well-being and personal improvement. Make sure your resolutions have motive and aren't entirely dictated through tendencies or out of doors pressure.

five. Time-Bond

Every choice must have a focused period. As an opportunity to declaring, "I'll get healthy in the long run," make a final date for yourself, like, "lose 10 pounds in six months." Setting time limits makes subjects experience extra urgent and maintains your interest on your dreams. It guarantees that your resolutions are clean, workable, and regular along aspect your prolonged-term dreams and values. It additionally permits you to show your development, hold motivation, and feel the fulfillment that comes from engaging in your desires. SMART objectives offer you the functionality to transform your New Year's resolutions into concrete, attainable strategies for private development.

PHYSICAL HEALTH AND FITNESS

EXERCISING REGULARLY

Frequent exercise improves highbrow and bodily fitness similarly to one's preferred satisfactory of existence, which makes it a well-known preference for New Year's resolutions. A lot of humans use the start of the 12 months to make better physical video games, and regular exercising suits in nicely with goals for pressure comfort, weight manipulate, and health. The symbolic start of a latest twelve months encourages human beings to decide to fundamental an energetic way of existence.

Sleep And Stress Management

Getting enough sleep and managing stress are vital additives of powerful self-development. These elements are crucial in identifying your diploma of achievement in exciting your New Year's resolutions.

1. Sleep And Goal Attainment

Restoration and Recovery: Sleep is a fundamental natural hobby that allows the renewal and healing of your body and mind. You awaken feeling rejuvenated and organized to absorb your resolutions with extra electricity and concentration at the same time as you got enough proper sleep.

Cognitive Function: Memory, learning, and selection-making are some of the cognitive strategies which can be strongly correlated with sleep. Getting enough sleep improves your capability to prioritize, put together, and make smart picks—all of which is probably critical for the accomplishment of a clear up.

Emotional Resilience: Insufficient sleep can cause mood modifications, infection, and a decrease in emotional resilience. You can better control stress, failures, and the unavoidable problems that upward push up whilst trying to paste on your resolutions in case you get a respectable night time time's sleep.

Physical Health: The kingdom of one's body is notably stimulated with the resource of the usage of sleep. It facilitates your immune device, regulates hormones, and aids in weight control—all of which is probably essential for your modern-day nicely-being and may have an impact at the accomplishment of fitness-associated resolutions.

2. Stress Reduction And Achieving Objectives

Better Decision-Making: Mindfulness and meditation are two effective stress-bargain strategies that let you make calm, sensible options even in hard situations. Having this to be had might be pretty beneficial even as making resolutions.

Improved Focus: Stress can cause distractions and intervene together with your capability to recognition. Stress manipulate permits you stay extra targeted on your goals and the movements required to get them.

Resilience In The Face Of Setbacks: Developing oneself is a direction fraught with disturbing situations and setbacks. Resilience is a capability that comes from effective stress control; it allows you to triumph over setbacks and preserve your determination to your desires.

Enhanced Productivity: Stress cut price has the capablity to decorate output. You're more likely to finish topics fast and stay together with your resolutions while you are not pressured with the aid of fear.

Better Habits: Stress can cause unhealthful coping strategies like emotional consuming or skipping out on self-care. You can develop healthful conduct that assist your resolutions through way of studying a way to manipulate pressure.

Long-run Well-Being: Stress cut rate techniques foster intellectual and emotional fitness, it truly is essential for contentment over the long term and the accomplishment of desires.

MENTAL AND EMOTIONAL WELL-BEING

PRACTICING MINDFULNESS AND MEDITATION

Choosing to consist of mindfulness and meditation into your New Year's plans is a notable step toward enhancing your intellectual and emotional fitness. These age-antique techniques, which have their roots in information, have many advantages which can beautify many components of your lifestyles. Meditation and mindfulness are beneficial inside the following methods:

1. Stress Management

Mindfulness: Mindfulness is the workout of dwelling within the present moment with out passing judgment on something. It will can help you allow pass of fears about the beyond and future, that can drastically relieve pressure. You collect the ability to stand issues with composure and tranquility.

Meditation: Consistently strolling in the direction of meditation allows decrease the frame's manufacturing of strain chemical materials like cortisol. Effective strain manage is primarily based upon on selling relaxation and triggering the body's relaxation response.

2. Better Mental Well-Being

Mindfulness: By elevating your degree of awareness of your thoughts and emotions, mindfulness will permit you to experience higher mentally. It lets in you address tension, melancholy, and other emotional difficulties with the beneficial useful resource of allowing you to look them objectively.

Meditation: Through enhancing self-attention, emotional regulation, and self-compassion, meditation fosters emotional nicely-being. It can help you in cultivating a happier mind-set on life.

3. Increased Productivity and Focus

Mindfulness: Mindfulness improves hobby and awareness with the useful resource of coaching your thoughts to live within the gift 2d. Working closer to your dreams may be made tons less complex with the aid of the usage of the improved productiveness that could quit end result from this heightened attention.

Meditating regularly improves your functionality to attention on obligations even within the presence of distractions. It might also moreover moreover bring about extra green selections and higher output.

four. Goal Specificity and Dedication

Mindfulness: By encouraging introspection and self-recognition, mindfulness permit you to in defining your dreams and aspirations. Connecting alongside side your requirements and the incentive inside the back of your resolutions becomes a whole lot less complicated as a surrender give up result.

Meditation: This workout develops strength of thoughts and patience, crucial dispositions for keeping your resolutions. It promotes a strain for self-improvement and a experience of cause.

5. Sturdy Emotional Base

Mindfulness: Mindfulness will let you grow to be greater emotionally resilient with the aid of training your thoughts to be present and non-reactive. You're extra capable of enduring the highs and lows of emotion that might accompany making resolutions.

Meditation: By supplying you with a better knowledge of your feelings, meditation allows you to react to barriers and disappointments greater deftly. Being emotionally conscious can assist with adaptability and resilience.

6. Improved Rest

Mindfulness: Mindfulness can help lessen racing thoughts and anxieties that regularly intrude with sleep. Better sleep is crucial for wellknown fitness, and it could be facilitated with the aid of a calmer thoughts.

Meditation: You may have a deeper, more restful sleep and discover it less complicated to nod off with the usage of meditation techniques, specially people who emphasize relaxation.

Emotional Quotient

Emotional intelligence, usually shortened to EQ, is a essential and complicated aspect of private improvement. Committing to enhancing your comprehension, manage, and dating collectively along with your very own feelings further to the ones of others is known as making emotional intelligence a New Year's decision. Empathy, electricity of thoughts, self-recognition, and sturdy interpersonal skills are all important. Additionally, take into account the subsequent factors:

1. Self-attention: Being able to choose out out and recognize your emotions is step one in developing emotional intelligence. You can apprehend your emotional triggers, patterns, and reactions through being more self-conscious. Because it allows you fit your goals and resolutions along with your underlying values and targets, self-reflected photo is crucial to creating significant goals and resolutions.

2. Self-Regulation: Among the vital additives of emotional intelligence is self-law,

or the skillful manipulate of your emotional reactions. Better self-law makes it lots much less complex a great way to stay composed underneath strain, chorus from making snap picks, and address difficult conditions. When walking on resolutions which could run into limitations or setbacks, that is precious.

3. Empathy: Empathy is the capacity to apprehend and experience a few different character's emotions. Empathy building is a vital trouble of emotional intelligence because it promotes improved communique between humans. Making empathy a subject improves your functionality to recognize the desires, desires, and feelings of others, that is first-rate in each private and expert contexts.

4. Social Skills: Another essential issue of emotional intelligence is the capability to efficiently have interaction with others. Deciding to paintings on your social abilties assist you to interact with human beings greater efficaciously, talk extra successfully, and boom sturdy bonds with them. This is

beneficial on your career, relationships with own family, and friendships, amongst exclusive regions of your lifestyles.

five. Conflict Resolution: Pursuing your resolutions frequently involves resolving disagreements. You can approach disagreements with a greater composed and beneficial attitude if you very personal emotional intelligence. You'll be more capable of resolving conflicts, establishing not unusual ground, and preserving healthy relationships—all of which can be important for carrying out your desires.

Chapter 3: Skill Development

LEARNING NEW SKILLS

Deciding to accumulate new capabilities in your New Year's decision is a powerful assertion of dedication in your improvement. It displays a force for facts growth, capability expansion, and self-development. This choice can take many certainly one of a type office work, which consist of learning a latest language, becoming gifted in an device, growing new interests, or enhancing one's expert competencies.

A lifetime of gaining knowledge of and private development can stop result from adopting a studying attitude, it's far a crucial thoughts-set. Challenges emerge as opportunities, mistakes come to be classes determined, and feedback turns into gas for private improvement if you have a boom attitude.

Challenges are thrilling rather than horrifying whilst one has a analyzing mind-set, which fosters a love of mastering and resilience that is essential for incredible accomplishment.

A reading thoughts-set encompasses an awful lot extra than a specific difficulty of view. It's approximately stepping outside of your consolation quarter and searching out new getting to know possibilities to region your coins in which your thoughts is.

Being uncomfortable is a vital a part of having a learning mind-set, because it's beyond your comfort region that actual boom and gaining knowledge of arise. Consider what clean obligations you may accomplish. Maybe choosing up a new talent, assuming a awesome feature, or doing a little element you have got in no way finished earlier than.

You have to studies and develop in a million and one strategies, and you may deal with a million and one challenges. To assist you in concentrating your efforts, it's far essential to create a gaining knowledge of and development plan.

Begin via thinking about your goals for the subsequent three hundred and sixty five days and the competencies and traits you may want to achieve them. Then you could decide which areas want improvement and which ones must be reinforced. This will assist you in figuring out your primary regions for development. Limit your development regions to two or three; in any other case, you run the risk of turning into overly distracted. Consider the goals and academic sports activities activities for the upcoming three, six, and 3 hundred and sixty five days for every development place.

It's notable, in my view, to set apart fine time for studying and development in preference to seeking to healthful it in at some stage in random hours. Consider even as you can carve out precise time for non-public improvement. You can also, as an example, agenda a ordinary duration to artwork earlier than or after your workday, or maybe include it into your workweek. You can inspire a studying mindset in your self through the use of way of making plans your day. Consider your desires, how you could locate time for private increase and mastering, and the way you could technique each day to exceptional accomplish them.

Importance of gaining expertise of new abilties

Lifelong Learning: The idea of lifelong reading is embodied in the purchase of latest abilities. It encourages increase mindsets, adaptability, and interest—trends which is probably essential in our dynamic worldwide.

Personal Growth: Learning new talents may be a catalyst for personal development and self-discovery. It pushes you to conquer troubles, get from your comfort area, and make more potent your resilience.

Cognitive Benefits: Learning improves cognitive feature through stimulating the mind. It improves essential wondering, memory, and trouble-fixing abilties—all of which is probably beneficial in lots of factors of lifestyles.

Career Advancement: Learning new abilities can enhance your opportunities of landing a interest if your choice is expert development. Promotions, pay increases, or new paintings potentialities have to give up result from it.

Creative Expression: Developing creative or revolutionary capabilities, along side writing, portray, or gambling an tool, offers a channel for one's creativity and self-expression.

Enhanced Confidence: Your self perception will increase as you come to be gifted in new competencies. Reaching dreams and gaining knowledge of new abilties allow you to enjoy more confident and well approximately yourself.

Problem Solving: Critical wondering and trouble-fixing are often required at the same time as gaining knowledge of new talents. These abilities will will let you end up a higher strategist and selection-maker in a single-of-a-type spheres of your existence.

Adaptability: Acquiring new capabilities increases your functionality for change. It promotes adaptability and an open mind, characteristics that is probably crucial for overcoming obstacles and transitions in existence.

Personal Fulfillment: You may revel in satisfied and fulfilled while you pursue pursuits and passions that healthy your abilties. It offers a happy and pleasing deliver.

Social Connection: Acquiring new abilties could probably result in social interplay opportunities. To make new buddies and contacts, you may join up in groups, commands, or agencies which might be associated with the information you have got were given decided on.

Time control: You regularly need to manipulate it gradual well to accumulate new abilities. Improved time manipulate talents can benefit you in many areas of your lifestyles.

Lifelong Adventure: Life will become a non-forestall journey at the same time as one gadgets out at the direction of obtaining new capabilities. It sustains your motivation, enthusiasm, and feel of purpose for the destiny.

Improving Existing Skills

Improving modern-day abilties is a profitable interest that might result in every profession and personal improvement. The following movements will help you in developing and honing your skills:

1. Self-Assessment: Start by using the use of identifying your present diploma of expertise. Determine your benefits and disadvantages inside the skill you choice to beautify. Your efforts to beautify can be guided via using this self-consciousness.

2. Establish Specific, Measurable, And Achievable Goals: Establish smooth goals to help you enhance your talents. Having particular dreams lets in you live stimulated and on course.

3. Ongoing Education: Look for equipment that will help you examine and get

better. This can involve reading books, taking on-line education, attending seminars, or asking mentors and difficulty-rely professionals for advice.

4. Consistent Practice: To enhance and hone your capabilities, exercise regularly. The mystery to improvement is consistency. Set aside time to exercise your abilities every day or each week.

five. Get Feedback: Encouragement to accumulate useful criticism from mentors or exclusive specialists within the area. You might not be capable of see areas for improvement on your private, however remarks can assist.

6. Adaptability: Show flexibility in the way you gift your case. To get higher, you may every now and then need to regulate your strategies or approaches. Try new topics and do not be scared to make errors so that you can enhance.

7. Mistakes and Failures: View errors and setbacks as opportunities for development and getting to know. They can provide insightful recommendation and assist you in honing your competencies.

eight. Seek Challenges: Set yourself up for success thru taking over assignments or initiatives that name if you want to comply with your competencies in novel and innovative approaches.

9. Time Management: Make the maximum of it gradual with the aid of allocating enough hours for potential improvement. Make mastering and exercising training a problem.

10. Remain Informed: Keep abreast of the maximum state-of-the-art improvements and inclinations with n the organization about your location of expertise. This guarantees the continuing applicability of your abilties and expertise considering understanding is electricity.

eleven. Networking: Make contacts with individuals who are informed within the discipline or who have comparable hobbies. Through networking, you could discover new thoughts, collaborate, and trade statistics.

12. Document Progress: Maintain a log of your upgrades. Keep a record of your successes, benchmarks, and regions for development. This can encourage you and make you feel happy with the direction you have got were given taken.

13. Mentorship: Seek a mentor who can offer path, mind-set, and a chance to exchange testimonies. Your tool of growing new abilties can be expedited with a mentor.

14. Celebrate Your Success: No depend how tiny, understand and honor your accomplishments. Acknowledging your development can boom yourself assure and strain.

15. Reflect and Adjust: Take time to endure in thoughts how you have got

advanced your abilties. Evaluate what's and is not going for walks. Adapt your goals and strategies for that reason.

Professional Development: A Comprehensive Overview

The approach of continuously improving and growing one's data, competencies, and capabilities to succeed in one's profession or career is called professional improvement. It is essential to each professional and private development because it permits humans to attain their desires and remain aggressive in a activity market that is usually converting.

An outline of professional development is supplied beneath:

1. Lifelong Learning: A self-control to lifelong reading is what professional development is all about. It's essential to stay modern and relevant inside the ever-converting worldwide of in recent times. This consists of continuously searching out possibilities to analyze new matters, hone

modern-day abilties, and alter to changes in the agency.

2. Skill Enhancement: A key difficulty of expert development is growing new skills and improving present day ones. Technical knowledge, manage, communique, hassle-fixing, and distinctive capabilities can all be taken into consideration a part of this.

3. Work Advancement: Getting expert improvement permit you to waft up the work ladder. Promotions, pay will increase, and the hazard to tackle extra responsibility at art work are all possible outcomes.

4. Goal Achievement: It assists people in expertise their desires and goals for their careers. Professional improvement offers humans the abilties and statistics they need to take a look at their dreams, whether or not or no longer they need to launch a business corporation, increase to a leadership characteristic, or emerge as an expert in a particular subject.

Chapter 4: Personal Growth
READING AND EDUCATION

Choosing to encompass analyzing and schooling in your New Year's resolutions is a commitment to lifelong learning, highbrow development, and personal improvement. This remedy covers an extensive style of options, at the side of analyzing more books, going to high school, or gaining information of recent subjects.

You will advantage from studying and schooling in the following strategies.

1. Intellectual Stimulation- Reading books, taking instructions, and the usage of self-have a look at property can all stimulate the mind. It sharpens your mind, extends your horizons, and develops critical thinking competencies.

2. Expanded Knowledge- Education and reading are powerful method of reading new matters. This decision expands your horizons whether or not you're studying approximately

new subjects, reading data, or staying up to date with the most contemporary improvements to your area.

three. Problem-Solving - Education and reading enhance your functionality to remedy problems. Applying knowledge from education lets in you to benefit data, draw instructions from the studies of others, and come up with unique solutions.

four. Empowerment - You in the in the meantime are able to take fee of your education and personal growth manner to this decision. You are free to choose what you have a look at or take a look at following your goals and regions of hobby.

five. Personal Growth - Education and analyzing promote non-public improvement and self-development. They can enhance your verbal exchange talents, assist you boom emotional intelligence, and assist you recognize yourself better.

6. Employment Enhancement - Education allow you to collect records and capabilities that could enhance your employment possibilities. Ongoing education is a first rate benefit whether or not or no longer you need to replace careers or develop to your modern one.

7. Cultural Awareness: Reading introduces you to lots of worldviews, cultures, and factors of view. This improves your empathy and cultural expertise, which enables you have got interaction with others from first-rate backgrounds.

eight. Personal Fulfillment - Reading and getting to know can result in a profound enjoy of contentment and happiness on a private degree. Learning new topics and enhancing oneself are intrinsically gratifying endeavors.

nine. Role Modeling - You set a excellent example for others with the aid of the usage of prioritizing expertise and studying. People spherical you may be inspired to examine as plenty as you are thru your self-discipline to it.

10. Creativity And Innovation - Reading and schooling can reveal you to a big form of ideas and ideas, that can foster your modern and innovative wondering. It inspires you to research novel options and cope with troubles from numerous views.

eleven. Constant Adaptation - Reading and schooling assist you live flexible and organized to deal with moving societal norms, technological enhancements, and inclinations in a global this is continuously converting.

12. Legacy Building: The records and capabilities you pick out up can become part of your legacy. Giving out your understanding and enjoy to others may additionally have an extended-lasting impact.

Building Self-Confidence

Gaining self-self assure is a awesome issue, however it takes time and effort—it does no longer take place .

To do that, you want to take the subsequent moves:

1. Establish Attainable Objectives: Divide your aspirations for self-warranty into extra sensible, smaller duties that may not appear too hard for you to complete. Reaching the ones desires will give you greater self-guarantee.

2. Positive Self-Talk: Swap out poor thoughts for affirmations which may be excellent. Stop concentrating on your mistakes and start reminding yourself of your accomplishments within the past.

3. Take Care Of Yourself: Maintain a healthy diet plan, get enough sleep, and interact in physical and highbrow interest to preserve your body and mind in accurate shape.

four. Get Out Of Your Comfort Zone: Take on new duties and endeavors, in spite of the fact that they first of all make you uncomfortable.

You can increase and benefit self guarantee from this.

five. Surround Yourself With Positive People: Create a network of mentors and friends who guide your development and agree with to your capability to carry out your resolution for the contemporary three hundred and sixty five days.

6. Keep A Journal: Record your development, successes, and instances of self-guarantee. Regularly take inventory of your journey.

RELATIONSHIPS

STRENGTHENING FRIENDSHIPS AND FAMILY BONDS

Consider those areas if you're seeking out to decide out a manner to spend more time at the side of your pals, family, or relationships;

Expressing affection to others.

Discussing our shared future.

Offering encouragement to others

Making time for every one of a kind and prioritizing the relationship; • Having enjoyment on the identical time as wearing out a laugh sports activities.

Many human beings are in a fulfillment relationships already, so that may be a exceptional manner to capitalize to your blessings and maintain your remedy to region your relationship first. These wholesome dating practices and interactions can therefore decorate your fitness. Being capable to expose someone you want them is useful to each events as it has an instantaneous impact on their health.

The fine technique to begin these own family or social resolutions is to talk with the human beings you need to spend extra time with and collaborate with them to parent out a way to make that appear. If there may be a third birthday celebration worried in these resolutions, you could discuss the choice and collaborate to establish a manner. Let's begin with smooth communique: What do you need to do? What are the various methods you can carry out the ones duties collectively?

People can enhance their preferred fitness, from mental nicely-being to bodily and behavioral blessings, by manner of means of making the aware choice to spend extra time with the people they love. More time spent with cherished ones can help lessen signs and signs and symptoms of melancholy, fear, and tension, similarly to feelings of isolation or loneliness. Similar to this, happier relationships are associated with better natural functioning, which incorporates decreased strain hormones, decreased contamination, and advanced cardiovascular fitness. Better sleep, a discounted hazard of contamination, and more healthy behavior are remarkable blessings. Trying workout instructions together or taking aspect in greater sports sports with cherished ones can sell greater wholesome conduct.

On the opportunity hand, lofty New Year's resolutions are not always difficult to break. You should right away textual content or cellphone your own family to let them understand you are thinking of them and time desk time together on their calendar if you find out yourself wavering for your remedy to spend greater time with them. Although scheduling the whole thing may not be proper, it is probably beneficial in a busy existence. We on occasion have to devise sports we enjoy with the human beings we like to healthful them in due to the reality we've got got so many obligations each day, like looking after circle of relatives individuals, jogging, and having youngsters.

If your resolutions do now not education consultaticn, it's far although crucial to address yourself and your family with kindness. Be supportive and there for each other, particularly if you want assistance regaining recognition or improving your objectives.

Communication Skills

As a New Year's choice, working on your courting's communication talents is a dedication to enhancing the way you and your companion interact. This resolution calls for attentive listening, eloquent and sympathetic expression of ideas and feelings, and wonderful dispute agreement. You can sell comprehension, emotional connection, and a happier, more healthy dating via the use of the use of emphasizing conversation. It's an essential intention for your dating's prolonged-time period fitness in addition to a profitable task for man or woman and interpersonal improvement.

Resolving Disputes

Declaring warfare selection as your New Year's choice shows that you are devoted to confronting and resolving disagreements in a extra effective manner in all facets of your lifestyles.

1. Better Connections: You may also moreover decorate your connections with own family, friends, and coworkers thru gaining knowledge of the manner to solve conflicts and misunderstandings.

2. Decreased Stress: Since unresolved conflicts may be a primary deliver of hysteria and anxiety, effective war preference can reduce pressure ranges.

three. Personal Growth: Gaining battle decision talents can be a journey of self-popularity and personal development on the way to beautify your comprehension of your emotions and responses.

4. Productivity: In the administrative center, powerful dispute choice can sell stronger collaboration, better output, and a happier surroundings.

5. Peace of Mind: Feeling assured and comfortab e ought to in all likelihood come from expertise that you are capable of managing conflict.

6.   Long-Term Benefits: Resolving disputes can forestall them from lingering and developing into large stressful situations down the road.

Financial Planning

BUDGETING AND SAVING

A prudent financial decision that would bring about extended financial protection and balance is to set a goal for your self this New Year to rate range and keep money. Here's an in depth breakdown of techniques and why this resolution is some thing you want to do not forget:

Why Saving and Budgeting Are Important

1.   Financial Security: By developing an emergency fund and maintaining coins, you could shield yourself financially in the occasion of surprising expenses or crises.

2.   Debt Reduction: Setting up an green budget lets in you to set aside coins for debt

reimbursement, which lowers interest fees and economic stress.

3. Achieving Goals: With financial savings, you could art work within the route of numerous financial goals, which include home ownership, business enterprise startup, and retirement training.

four. Peace of Mind: Having economic economic financial savings and know-how in which your coins is going may also help ease financial uncertainty-related fear.

How To Put Saving And Budgeting Into Practice As A New Year's Resolution:

1. Set Clearly Defined Financial Objectives: Specify your economic savings and budgetary desires. This may be putting in vicinity an emergency fund, clearing debt, or placing apart cash for a selected purpose.

2. Create a Budget: Make an intensive rate range that money owed for all of your prices in addition to your income. You also can screen your expenses and find out

locations wherein you can make savings thru doing this.

3. Track Expenses: Whether you operate a spreadsheet or an app for budgeting, maintain a record of the whole thing you spend. You'll get an understanding of your spending patterns as a surrender stop result.

four. Prioritize Savings: Make saving a fixed sum of money each month. Set apart a number of your profits for economic financial financial savings in advance than you spend it on non-critical objects.

five. Reduce Needless Expenses: Examine your spending plan to discover fees that may be lessen or eliminated. This can be reducing over again on eating out, terminating subscriptions that aren't being used, or seeking out less high priced alternatives.

6. Automate Savings: Establish normal deposits into a specific monetary savings account. It lets in you to have coins regularly.

7. Observe and Modify: Review your economic economic financial savings and fee variety often. As crucial, make adjustments to live on direction for your goals.

8. Ask for Expert Advice: Seek the recommendation of a monetary expert when you have any questions about making an funding your monetary monetary financial savings or growing a fee variety.

Benefits Of Budgeting And Saving

1. Financial Freedom: Reaching your monetary economic savings desires will provide you the freedom to make alternatives while not having to worry about coins.

2. Decreased tension: Having a properly-defined economic plan and a protection net can appreciably reduce the fear and tension associated with cash.

three. Building Wealth: Consistent saving and making an investment through the years can bring about the purchase of wealth and financial freedom.

4. Improved Financial Discipline: Budgeting fosters financial obligation and project, that may have an top notch impact on all components of your lifestyles.

5. Extended-Duration Security: Being nicely-prepared for the future is ensured with the aid of planning for retirement or sudden goals.

Reducing Debt

Making debt discount a pinnacle precedence for the brand new 12 months is a large and accountable financial preference. Here's an extensive breakdown of the reasons within the once more of and strategies for accomplishing this cause:

Why Debt Reduction Is Important

1. Economic Liberty: Less financial pressure outcomes from debt discount, imparting you with more monetary freedom to make decisions and manipulate your charge range without being confined with the useful resource of manner of debt.

2. Improved Credit Score: Paying off debt can also have a effective effect for your credit rating rating, in order to make it simpler and greater much less costly to advantage credit score within the destiny

three. Interest Savings: Reducing debt permits you to hold cash on hobby bills, which you could then use for investments, economic savings, or unique financial dreams.

four. Reduction of Stress: Debt is a prime cause of stress. Reducing it eases economic anxiety and promotes intellectual tranquility.

5. Economic Sustainability: A sound monetary existence need to include debt control and cut price because it creates the foundation for wealth accumulation.

How To Make Debt Reduction A New Year's Resolution

Evaluate Your Debt: Make a listing of all the money you owe, including loans, credit rating card payments, and particular debts. A be aware ought to be manufactured from the hobby prices, minimum, and total quantities due.

Establish a Plan for Repayment: Create an intensive plan outlining your debt repayment method. Select a debt control plan, which incorporates the debt avalanche, which will pay off the loans with the very great hobby prices first, or the debt snowball, that may pay off the smallest debts first.

Set Realistic Goals: Create viable benchmarks for debt discount. These objectives may be set as quarterly, every 12 months, or month-to-month goals.

Reduce Needless Costs: Look over your spending plan to find out locations in which you may cut decrease again. Invest the coins you keep inside the route of paying off debt.

Increase Income: Seek out ways to boom your profits, collectively with selling assets you no longer need, taking on element-time artwork, or freelancing.

Prioritize High-Interest Debt: Since excessive-hobby money owed have the ability to accrue more hobby through the years, supply them priority in relation to reimbursement.

Avoid Creating New Debt: As you attempt to lower your gift responsibilities, decide to chorus from taking on in addition debt.

Establish an Emergencies Fund: Concurrently, task to installation an emergency fund to cope with surprising expenses. By doing this, it can be feasible to keep away from the use of credit score rating playing cards in times of want.

Ask for Expert Advice: Think approximately getting assistance from a financial representative or credit score score rating counselor if your debt state of affairs is complex or overwhelming.

Benefits of Reducing Debt

Financial Liberty: Your ability to make alternatives primarily based for your possibilities in area of your duties increases as you pay off debt.

Reduced Stress: Financial pressure and anxiety are decreased while there is much less debt.

Interest Savings: Over time, you may preserve a exquisite amount of money thru putting off immoderate-interest loans.

Better Credit Score: Lowering debt will enhance your credit rating score score, that would let you take gain of more economic alternatives.

Enhanced Financial Security: Debt cut price is a vital first step towards amassing wealth and making sure lengthy-term monetary safety.

Retirement And Investing Planning

A prudent and astute monetary remedy might be to make your New Year's selection supply interest to growing an funding and retirement making plans. Here's an intensive breakdown of the reasons inside the lower again of and techniques for attaining this purpose:

Why Retirement Planning And Investment Matters

Financial Security: Retirement making plans and investments guarantee you've got got a protection net on your cash in later existence, reducing the possibility of handling monetary issues in retirement.

Building Wealth: You can boom your wealth over time with sensible investments, supplying you with the cash you need to acquire your economic objectives and live certainly.

Readiness for Retirement: Making a plan in your retirement ensures that you may have sufficient cash to revel in your golden years with out relying genuinely on Social Security or special authorities assist.

Efficient Taxation: You can keep extra of your earnings by using minimizing your tax legal duty with the beneficial aid of cautious retirement making plans.

Peace of Mind: You would possibly revel in an awful lot much less forced approximately coins and further confident about your financial future with the resource of way of getting cautiously considered retirement and making an investment plans.

How To Put Retirement And Investing Planning Into Practice As A New Year's Resolution

Clearly define your retirement dreams. Establish your retirement age and the manner of life you preference to guide. This will assist you in figuring out how an awful lot you need to set apart.

Chapter 5: Time Management
SETTING PRIORITIES

Making the most of it gradual and belongings and focusing on the matters which might be essential in lifestyles may be finished via committing to set priorities as a New Year's selection. An outline for creating and adhering to priorities is supplied under:

Why Prioritization Is Important

Effective Time Management: Setting priorities allows you popularity your effort and time at the maximum crucial responsibilities and desires, which enhances output.

Goal Achievement: Setting priorities enables you hobby at the topics which may be most important to you, whether or not or not they have to do together with your health, career, or non-public life.

Decreased Stress: By supporting you in specializing in what is important and avoiding distractions, putting priorities will let you enjoy much less crushed and compelled.

Focus and Clarity: It enables you're making alternatives which is probably constant together with your goals by way of the use of manner of offering you with clarity approximately your ideals and your chosen results.

How to Put Creating Priorities as a New Year's Resolution into Practice

Introspection: Give your ideals, lengthy-term goals, and private priorities some idea. You can use this to decide what your top priorities are.

Make a list of your priorities: Make a list of the topics which is probably maximum critical to you, considering your lengthy- and quick-term desires in unique factors of your existence (e.G., career, own family, health, non-public growth).

Set SMART Goals: Convert your priorities into SMART desires—specific, measurable, practical, applicable, and time-certain. They turn out to be trackable and actionable as a cease end result.

Time Management: Make a timetable or time manipulate technique that enables you awareness your interest at the matters which can be maximum vital to you. Don't fill your time table an excessive amount of with unimportant subjects.

Eradicate Distractions: Recognize and decrease down on any distractions that would draw your interest a long way from your top priorities. This can entail putting in limits on the usage of era or spending plenty a lot much less time on unimportant obligations.

Remain Adjustable: Prioritizing matters is fundamental, but you moreover can also need to be flexible sufficient to shift path whilst needed.

Monitor Development: Analyze your improvement in the route of your pinnacle priorities regularly, and make any critical plan adjustments.

Benefits of Setting Priorities

Increased Productivity: You can do more duties in tons less time if you cope with your pinnacle priorities.

Goal Achievement: Setting priorities ensures which you pass forward step by step in conjunction with your maximum important goals.

Reduced Stress: It lessens the feel of being overburdened and aids in inexperienced undertaking manipulate.

Improved Decision-Making: Having a clear framework to manual your options whilst you set priorities permits choice-making.

Better Work-Life Harmony: Setting priorities can help you balance your private and artwork lives and prevent burnout.

Details and Objective: It permits you're making picks which can be ordinary along side your values through giving your existence course and a enjoy of motive.

Balancing Life And Work

Setting a goal for the New Year to stability paintings and life is admirable considering the truth that it may increase happiness and great properly-being. Here's a manner to efficiently set and achieve this motive:

Why It's Important To Balance Life And Work

Well-Being And Health: For both mental and physical health, a piece-existence stability is crucial. It lessens anxiety and keeps burnout at bay.

Quality Relationships: Maintaining a healthful art work-lifestyles stability lets in you to assemble and maintain deep bonds with buddies and circle of relatives.

Enhanced Efficiency: Taking care of your very own dreams and interests let you be more innovative and green at artwork.

Self-Care: It guarantees which you have time for sports such as workout, relaxation, and appealing in interests and pursuits.

How to Make Work-Life Balancing a New Year's Resolution

Establish Limits: Define splendid obstacles among your personal and expert lives. Establish easy guidelines for non-public and paintings hours.

Prioritize Self-Care: Include regular exercising, relaxation, and amusement activities on your schedule to show your self that you price your well-being.

Time Management: Make the most of your work hours and steer clean of overworking with the beneficial aid of the usage of efficient time manage strategies.

Delegate And Say No: Develop the capacity to show down assignments at work and decline take-on at the same time as your plate is already complete.

Quality Time With Family And Friends: Make time to your calendar to spend at the side of your circle of relatives and make massive connections.

Digital Detox: To absolutely detach from paintings, restriction the amount of time you spend on social media and digital devices in the path of your unfastened time.

Plan Vacations: Make positive you're taking regular breaks and holidays to rejuvenate and spend treasured time with cherished ones.

Communication: Make excellent your boss and coworkers are privy to your limitations with the aid of the use of the usage of sharing your aspirations for a bit-existence balance.

Benefits Of Balancing Work And Life

Reduced Stress: Living a balanced lifestyles improves mental and emotional fitness by means of reducing pressure and burnout.

Stronger Relationships: Making private time a trouble improves ties with friends and family.

Improved Productivity: You can be greater progressive and efficient at work when you have a piece-lifestyles stability.

Improved Health: It promotes sturdiness and massive properly-being with the resource of enhancing each mental and bodily fitness.

Self-Care: Maintaining a chunk-existence stability lets in you to interact in self-care sports activities that beautify your properly-being.

Fulfillment: Having a healthful paintings-existence stability will increase happiness and existence delight.

TRACKING AND MEASURING PROGRESS

KEEPING A RESOLUTION JOURNAL

Maintaining a New Year's preference notebook is a exceptional way to assess your goals, display your improvement, and hold motivation. To start and preserve up a resolution mag, observe the ones steps:

1. Selecting Your Journal

Whether it's an digital magazine or a traditional notepad, choose one which you enjoy using. Make advantageous you could live up for using it frequently.

2. Make Definite Goals

Record your desires for the approaching year inside the magazine. Give specifics approximately your desires and the motives they may be vital to you.

3. Establish A Timetable

Choose a everyday updating time table on your mag. It might be done on a every day, weekly, or monthly basis, based totally in your pastimes and goals.

four. Monitor Development

Continually file your improvement. Talk about your troubles in addition to your accomplishments. Be sincere with yourself.

five. Contemplate And Assess

Give your journey some idea. Analyze what's effective and what calls for change. Write down ability solutions inside the magazine.

6. Remain Inspired

Go lower lower back on your preliminary motivation for making the ones resolutions to your pocket e book. Write about your inspirations and include perception-frightening phrases or pix.

7. Celebrate Accomplishments

Keep a record of your successes and get satisfaction from the texture of achievement, have a laugh your self.

8. Take Advice From Failures

Record your magazine entries concerning any hurdles or setbacks you experience. Examine what went wrong and the way you may possibly manage comparable conditions within the future.

nine. Take Responsibility For Yourself

You can use your magazine as a device to keep your self responsible. To make certain you are remaining on direction, periodically assessment your targets and development.

10. Provide Images

To decorate the visible splendor of your diary and to greater efficaciously show your development, encompass snap shots, graphs, or charts.

11. Tell About Your Trip

Think approximately showing a pal or relative who is encouraging you to read your resolve pocket e-book. They can useful resource you and preserve you responsible.

12. Exercise Persistence And Patience

Recall that transformation requires time. Remind your self of your dedication and your accomplishments via using your mag. Never surrender.

thirteen. Modify Your Objectives

It is suitable to adjust your dreams all through the yr if your priorities shift. Make those modifications on your magazine and, if crucial, write new dreams.

14. Maintain Uniformity

Consistency is vital even as retaining a treatment pocket book. As you enlarge the exercise of journaling, it will in the end play a vital position in helping you satisfy your resolutions.

You can correctly music your improvement, preserve motivation, and lift your chances of undertaking your goals via retaining a New Year's decision pocket e-book. It's an powerful device for developing oneself and improving oneself.

Using Apps And Tools

A useful tip for remaining prompted and prepared is to track your New Year's resolutions using gear and packages. Here's a way to apply those net belongings efficiently, step-via-step:

Selecting Appropriate Apps And Tools

Begin via deciding on tools and applications that complement your particular goals. Think about the desires you have for your self, which consist of improving your productivity, income, bodily fitness, or non-public increase.

Specify Your Objectives Clearly

Specify your goals for the new yr. Progress monitoring and size can be much less complex as a forestall give up end result.

Divide Objectives Into Doable Steps

Break down each reason into greater feasible jobs or steps. This facilitates you higher music your improvement and makes it greater plausible.

Utilize Apps For Setting Goals

Make use of cause-placing packages which includes "Todoist," "Trello," "Asana," or "GoalsOnTrack" to set up goals and assign obligations. These apps often provide reminder and last date-placing functions.

Apps For Habit-Tracking

Use dependancy-monitoring applications along with "HabitBull," "Streaks," or "Habitica" for goals which consist of growing new conduct or breaking gift ones. You can maintain an eye constant to your every day development with these apps.

Apps For Calendars And Reminders

Include your desires and pertinent obligations inside the calendar software program (such as Google Calendar or Apple Calendar). Make nice to allocate time specially for focusing in your resolutions and set commonplace reminders.

Journaling And Note-Taking Apps

Maintain an virtual mag by using the use of the use of programs which incorporates "Evernote," "OneNote," or "Day One." Keep a mag of your desires-associated mind, insights, and studies.

Tools For Project Management

Create undertaking boards and display your progress using mission manipulate system like "Notion," "Trello," or "Asana" if your dreams are complicated and require several steps or collaborators.

Apps For Monitoring Finances

If you have got got monetary goals, you may need to use apps like "Mint" or "You Need a Budget (YNAB)" to maintain track of your financial financial savings, create budgets, and screen your spending.

Apps For Fitness And Health

Apps like "MyFitnessPal," "Fitbit," or "Strava" can assist you in tracking your workout ordinary, nutritional intake, and general properly-being if your priorities are fitness and fitness.

Apps For Meditation And Mindfulness

Employ mindfulness and meditation programs such as "Headspace" or "Calm" to effectively manage strain and preserve a nicely-rounded perspective on the identical time as pursuing your targets.

Virtual Education Platforms

Check out online reading environments and courses on net sites like "Coursera," "Udemy," or "edX" if you want to observe new topics.

Establish Social Assistance

Use apps like "WhatsApp," "Slack," or "Facebook Groups" to join on-line companies or connect to friends to speak about your goals and improvement and get useful resource and responsibility.

Tools For Time Management

Utilize time control programs like "Focus@Will" or "RescueTime" to evaluate and enhance some time management practices and ensure they assist your targets.

Frequent Goal Assessment

Use a calendar or reminder gear to set up recurring opinions of your desires.

Throughout the ones critiques, evaluate your advancement, adjust your techniques, and hold obligation.

Security And Backup Of Data

Use password managers together with "LastPass" or "1Password" to stable your statistics and protect your payments.

You may moreover furthermore simplify the method of recording your New Year's resolutions, keep motivation, and enhance your possibilities of achievement through way of the use of adhering to those recommendations and making green use of the relevant machine and programs. Recall to preserve consistency and regulate your technique as you enhance.

Seeking guide and obligation

Getting help and retaining your self accountable is a extraordinary approach to preserve your New Year's resolutions on direction. Follow those steps:

Chapter 6: Overcoming Challenges And Relapses

DEALING WITH SETBACKS

Overcoming boundaries to wearing out New Year's resolutions is a critical step inside the gadget. Here are some tips for overcoming obstacles and persevering with to your path:

Remain upbeat and self-compassionate

Remain forgiving of yourself. Failures are an inevitable a part of chasing any intention. Continue to expect undoubtedly and with self-compassion. Recall that your whole development is not defined with the resource of a unmarried setback.

Examine and Interpret the Failure

Spend a while identifying what brought approximately the setback. Was it due to unanticipated occasions, a loss of strength, or an impractical goal? Effectively addressing the purpose can be facilitated with the beneficial useful resource of figuring out it.

Modify Your Objectives If Required

If you maintain experiencing setbacks, think about whether or now not your unique goals have been too lofty or unrealistic. To make your desires more potential, you can need to make a few changes.

Review Your Strategy

Go over your techniques and motion plan. Can you put into impact any changes to ward off such misfortunes within the destiny?

Look for Assistance and Responsibility

Speak along with your aid device or obligation partner. By speakme approximately your disasters, you car get preserve of insightful recommendation, supportive comments, and beneficial guidelines on a manner to get lower once more at the proper music.

Remain Dedicated

Failures do not same setbacks. Remember why engaging in your desires is vital to you and reaffirm your dedication to them. Remember your lengthy-time period desires.

Dissect It

Divide a top setback into smaller, extra viable tiers if it feels overwhelming. To regain your momentum, deal with transferring in advance one step at a time.

Turn Failures Into Learning Opportunities

See failures as a threat to decorate and observe. Think about the instructions you found from the failure and the way you could examine the ones to reinforce your future enhancements.

Put Resilience Into Practice

Develop resilience with the resource of figuring out that barriers are inevitable in life. Gaining resilience will allow you to triumph over boundaries with extra strength.

Maintain Consistency

The mystery to overcoming limitations is consistency. Eventually, fulfillment is feasible even inside the face of challenges in case you preserve to place up regular strive.

Establish Reasonable Expectations

Make high-quality your time limits and desires are affordable. Setbacks and disappointment could possibly cuit result from having unrealistic expectancies. Verify that your objectives can be met in slight of your current-day scenario.

Track Your Progress

Evaluate your development often and adapt as essential. You may additionally discover regions in which you need to exert extra strive with the aid of maintaining song of your improvement.

Honor Minor Victories

This ought to possibly help you live advocated and function a reminder of your accomplishments.

Maintain Your Tenacity

Reaching your desires won't usually comply with a immediately direction. Remain tenacious, focus at the intention, and do not allow disasters to demoralize you.

Look for Expert Assistance

Recall that boundaries are a stylish element of each direction inside the path of task goals. They can offer insightful data and opportunities for private improvement. You can use disasters as stepping stones closer to fulfillment in case you technique them with tenacity and an exquisite outlook.

Staying Motivated

Maintaining your passion and devotion to achieving your New Year's resolutions may be hard, however with the best techniques, it's far viable. This is a manner to preserve motivation:

Make precise, properly-described desires

Ensure that your resolutions are clean and specific. It's tons less hard to stay encouraged whilst your dreams are clear because of the truth that you recognize exactly what you are aiming for.

Divide Objectives Into Manageable Steps

Break your goals down into extra viable steps. This permits you got your goals greater without hassle and with less crush.

Produce A Graphical Layout

To help you envision your desires, make a imaginative and prescient board, use purpose-monitoring packages, or keep a physical development tracker. Observing your improvement may be pretty inspiring.

Make Use Of Encouragement Words

Create empowering statements about your goals. You can boom your motivation and self-guarantee with the resource of the use of repeating those affirmations every day.

Locate Your "Why

Recognize and keep in thoughts the motives that your dreams are big to you. When obstacles come your manner, remembering your "why" will help you stay prompted and focused.

Establish Due dates

Give your pastimes less steeply-priced timeframes. Setting very last dates can encourage motivation and a revel in of urgency.

Make It Enjoyable

Look for methods to characteristic amusement to the technique. Maintaining motivation is better at the same time as walking towards your goals is thrilling.

Be Accountable

To stay inspired and on course, rent an app or duty accomplice, or percentage your dreams with a friend.

Celebrate Significant Occasions

Acknowledge and admire every minor victory you've got were given alongside the manner. This encouragement will permit you to stay driven.

See Your Achievement

Take some time to have a look at your fulfillment. Imagine the sensation of carrying out your goals. Motivation can be increased via visualization.

Remove All Distractions

Recognize and reduce distractions that restrict your development. Establish a focused workspace to hold on direction.

Look For Motivation

Watch or be aware of podcasts, have a look at books, or watch movies about your targets. You can re-ignite your motivation via way of surrounding yourself with uplifting material.

Accept Challenges

View limitations as possibilities for personal improvement in desire to topics to keep away from. Overcoming setbacks can foster resilience and motivation.

Learn From Failures

Instead of seeing setbacks as failures, see them as possibilities for increase. Examine what went wrong and have a look at this records to alter your method.

Be Consistency

Long-term motivation calls for consistency. Maintain your habitual and your dedication, even at the times at the same time as you experience less inspired.

Modify as Required

Be willing to modify your desires or strategies in case you find that they are now not effective for you or in case your state of affairs significantly modifications.

Employ Social Assistance

Talk approximately your desires with buddies or get involved in a community or business enterprise of like-minded humans. Having a network of supporters may be inspiring and energizing.

Assign Novel Tasks

To preserve your self stimulated and increase for my part, create new desires when you've accomplished your modern-day ones.

Take Care of Yourself

Make self-care a issue to ensure you've got got got the physical and intellectual stamina to live encouraged. This includes consuming properly, controlling strain, and getting adequate sleep.

Examine and Consider

Regularly have a observe your development and take into account your path. This can assist your motivation and help you live on the course.

Although motivation can fluctuate, you could make your ordinary life extra inspiring with the useful resource of enforcing those techniques, which let you gain your New Year's resolutions.

Chapter 7: When And Why?

Why Do People Make New Year's Resolutions?

Too many, there may be a amazing appeal to growing a exchange on the begin of the current-day 12 months. New beginnings frequently signal a time for a sparkling start—a risk to put beyond errors in the back of and look to the future.

Having an entire 12 months ahead can feel like a clean slate, entire of opportunity and capability. When humans make extraordinary changes for the subsequent twelve months, furthermore they've a sense of manipulate.

Tradition has a detail as properly. As we are going to see, there may be a particular cultural factor for tremendous human beings thinking about the reality that resolutions had been made for masses generations.

But because of all of those factors, human beings are regularly below some of stress to make those changes, which can be one of the reasons of the excessive failure charge.

When Did New Year's Resolutions Begin?

The first regarded references to New Year's resolutions come from the historic Babylonians. The Babylonians celebrated the begin of the current yr and the sowing of flowers so long as 4,000 years inside the beyond. In an attempt to win the gods' need, they pledged to pay off debts and pass back any valuables that they had borrowed at the same time as reaffirming their allegiance to the monarch.

History furthermore shows us that the Romans had similar practices, and they eventually moved the calendar spherical so the one year began on January 1st. This coincided with the birthday celebration of the god Janus, who seemed decrease returned on the preceding three hundred and sixty five days and regarded earlier to the destiny. The Romans made ensures of proper behavior for the yr earlier.

While the concept of setting goals for the subsequent year is in large related to the West, other cultures have a look at comparable customs. For example, in Japan, a few human beings exercise Kakizome, wherein they write their cause for the 12 months beforehand in ornate calligraphy.

Even with their archaic origins, a whole lot of people however make goals each 12 months. For example, consistent with one survey, forty 4% of humans within the UK planned on making resolutions each year.

The Power of The New Year's Resolution

As the holidays approach and the New Year techniques, many human beings are thinking lower decrease again at the beyond and reevaluating a number of their alternatives. For folks who have no longer started out making the adjustments they promised to begin next week, subsequent month, or possibly whilst winter arrives, the New Year's resolutions offer the right chance. We'll percentage charming information regarding this choice with you on this submit and offer useful tips for developing with a prevailing list of goals for the following yr.

Nowadays, 45% of Americans make New Year's resolutions. While almost half of of all Americans make resolutions, 25% of them surrender on their resolutions with the useful useful resource of the second week of January.

New Year's resolutions variety spherical the world. Or at least, that's the notion you can draw from Google Maps venture known as Zeitgeist. Internet customers from around the world had been invited to percentage their resolutions. Google then mapped and evaluated them, classifying them into the subsequent domains: schooling, cash, career, love, and fitness.

Looking on the map, fitness-associated resolutions predominated within the US and Egypt. Visitors from Australia and Japan were seeking out love. In Russia, in the period in-between, schooling have become the pinnacle precedence. And in India, profession dreams had been dominant.

Of direction, that is a long way from a scientific have a take a look at, but it's no matter the fact that thrilling.

So, what had been the top New Year's resolutions? Social attempted to answer that question primarily based completely totally on customers' tweets. Here are the outcomes:

Save coins

Be a nicer human.

Get a modern approach.

Give more money and time to charity.

Drink a bargain much less

Diet, exercise, and weight reduction

Read greater

Learn something new.

Sleep extra

Make new buddies

Why Do New Year's Resolutions Fail?

Examining the reasons why it is probably tough so you can maintain your New Year's goals is one method that will help you recognize the way to make resolutions which you are in all likelihood to paste to.

These consist of:

1. You weren't in reality caused to gain your dreams due to the fact you have been now not that interested by doing so. This is often the case with New Year's resolutions, for the reason that they'll be usually movements we sense we need to do in desire to ones we like, now not that we need to do. Goals want to excite and inspire you, or you simply acquired't advantage them.

2. Your goals had been too bold; you may have struggled to comprehend wherein to begin or actually given up in depression at the size of the project.

three. Your dreams targeted on techniques, not consequences. It is a excellent deal less complicated to inspire ourselves to do something if we think about the final results we need to achieve, now not what we ought to do to get there. For instance, it is a extremely good deal tons less difficult to shop a bit bit extra even as you bear in mind the motive of your monetary savings—likely buying a domestic or a car.

four. Your dreams did no longer expand you closer to a more complete "life intention." You could not see how they had been going to help you get to wherein you without a doubt favored to be in lifestyles.

5. The timing of your goal have become not described, so there has been no incentive to get began. We regularly want some shape of 'kick-start' for personal change, and a time-positive motive can help.

6. You did no longer pause to take into account the moves you'll need to take a good

way to accomplish your targets. Having a clean idea of what you need to do is critical.

A speedy trying to find at the internet will provide loads of facts at the failure charge of resolutions. Whatever the end cease end result, it's usually pretty excessive. So why are people so horrific at finishing their every one year dreams?

There are a few capability reasons:

The objectives aren't precise sufficient. It's truly easy to be dubious on the identical time as making resolutions. 'Eat lots tons much less chocolate' or save extra cash' aren't in particular purpose-centered or measurable. What does greater or a high-quality deal an awful lot less appear to be? And over what time period? Finding the right trouble to clear up may be useful.

There are too many resolutions. Many humans skip too a long manner with the concept of a contemporary begin, compiling a list of their very own imagined crimes and seeking to seize up on every one. As soon as one goes via the wayside, it is able to be disheartening to maintain with the others.

It's tough to trade behaviors. Ultimately, New Year's resolutions are normally approximately converting behaviors. If you do no longer understand them and alter the mentality that fuels them, it is able to be tough to acquire this.

There's no responsibility. It's no longer continuously smooth to be self-accountable. Individuals are skilled at offering justifications or overlooking little errors. People hardly ever preserve their desires as an entire lot as others to keep them responsible.

It ought to, consequently, be easy that placing the right resolutions or dreams is an important a part of being able to preserve your New Year resolutions.

Chapter 8: The Personal Change Process

Any approach of private boom goes via those stages:

1.   Establishing your non-public goals and vision: figuring out in which you want to move in existence.

2.   Organizing your private growth entails figuring out the steps crucial to attain your goals and vision.

three. Starting to make modifications: in fact, doing something to transport within the course of your dreams.

four.   Evaluating your mastering as a manner to determine what you have got were given finished and what greater wants to be finished.

five.   Revising your plan if crucial to reflect your development or maybe changes on your vision and desires due to the reality of making changes.

In essence, New Year's resolutions are simply non-public aspirations or visions of who you need to be within the destiny. As such, they are simplest a part of the approach of bringing approximately personal improvement.

Although they constitute the start, they will be inadequate on their very very personal. There is also an art and a technology to putting a private imaginative and prescient and desires—and in case you do now not cause them to suitable, you could not discover them motivating enough to hold!

Making Personal Change: Developing New Habits

But what about whilst you anticipate you have got were given made the right resolutions? You started out out, you have been pushed, and also you installation time barriers, but why couldn't you find enough time?

Is there a few problem you can do approximately that? The solution is sure—and it lies in expertise how we expand new behavior (see container). It additionally includes continuing your willpower at the same time as accepting the uncommon slip-up.

The Science of Developing Habits

The adage "exercising makes awesome" is not new.

Few human beings ever genuinely acquire perfection, however there is absolute confidence that practice is vital to developing any new potential. It turns out that practice is essential to developing any new addiction, too.

Research indicates that we want to do a little aspect for approximately 20 hours earlier than it turns into a dependancy.

This is pleasant a ultra-current "rule of thumb," no longer an absolute: first rate humans and behavior take longer to shape, at the same time as others can do it more unexpectedly.

Chapter 9: How To Make New Year's Resolutions

Now permit s be privy to putting our very own resolutions for the following 12 months. First, allow's circulate over again to powerful goal-setting to get started out.

There are 5 standards of purpose-putting:

They want to be smooth.

They need to offer a motivating amount of project.

They must have the self-discipline of the person setting them

Feedback on development have to be taken under attention.

The complexity of the desired responsibilities need to be taken under attention.

So, going returned to one of the 'first rate' examples stated above, allow's turn it into a greater top notch one—exercising extra.

Rather than the use of the pretty popular word, permit's first define it. An grownup's advocated quantity of exercise is at the least 100 fifty mins of mild cardio hobby or seventy five mins of full of lifestyles aerobic interest each week. This is a incredible place to begin.

Let's now quantify and benefit it: in January, have interaction in at least 100 fifty minutes each week of slight workout. Once another time, there are many strategies to display your improvement on this vicinity, and the primary time frame is virtually short.

Your selection additionally wants to be relevant in your life, so you also can have a larger aim in mind. For example, you will likely assignment yourself to finish a 10-kilometer run thru April. This offers you with a concrete timeline and the opportunity to head toward your purpose, step by step.

By constructing your choice this manner, you may have a clean purpose with a motivating amount of venture. You're moreover showing dedication to the choice thru giving a agency date and allowing the danger for feedback on your development if you want to alter.

How Can I Make a Realistic New Year's Resolution That Will Work?

Almost 30% of human beings never make New Year's resolutions due to the fact they understand they may not be capable of hold them. On the opportunity hand, those who set resolutions for the New Year have a tenfold better danger of succeeding than parents that don't.

A strong method would possibly help you in resolving loads of troubles. It can also assist make your life exactly the way you want it to be. But developing a plan isn't always an clean project. Therefore, we've got got organized a few specific suggestions for you.

1. Summarize The Past Year

Possessing the proper thoughts-set is the first step closer to right planning. Take out your preferred pen and notepad, sit down down down down, and check the very last yr in phrases of your successes, setbacks, and new contacts.

If you moreover mght made a New Year's decision the previous twelve months, be sure to encompass it proper proper right here.

If you furthermore mght made a New Year's choice the previous year, make sure to embody it right here. How many dreams have you reached? Why haven't you been able to placed into impact one-of-a-type dreams? If you have had been given been setting the same goal for yourself for a few years but nevertheless can't make it come actual, likely you do not actually need it, and the intention is imposed by means of way of the surroundings or marketing.

2. Define The Concept of The Year

Before you begin the in-depth making plans, it is probably super if you could clearly united states your one primary intention for the three hundred and sixty five days. Also, in advance than placing any aim, make sure that this is precisely what you really want. It corresponds on your pursuits and goals.

three. Break Down Goals into Small Tasks

Try to check every purpose with the questions. Below, you can find out examples:

If the aim is not met, what is going to expose up?

What am I inclined to pay to satisfy it (time, attempt)?

What am I improving in myself and within the international via the use of conducting this purpose?

If the reason is without a doubt important, then wreck it down into precise obligations. For convenience, you may divide them into six conditional lists: "artwork," "family," "relationships," "money," "pursuits," and "non-public development.".

To make sure your dreams are clear and accessible, you may use the SMART method. It states that every of them should be:

Specific (smooth, sensible, large).

Measurable (meaningful, motivating).

Achievable (agreed, doable).

Relevant (low price, practical, and resourced; consequences-based without a doubt).

Time-tremendous (time-based, time-restrained, time/fee-confined, well timed, time-touchy)

four. Make a Plan For a Plan

Timely distribution of the subtasks is the first step toward beginning implementation. We propose making lists of duties for the month, week, and day with periodic reminders. You can use planner apps for smartphones, Google Calendar, paper lists, and plenty of others.

Of path, you could no longer have the potential to plot the complete twelve months through the hour, however it's far a possible task to outline a great plan and periodically pass back to it for clarifications.

5. Believe in Yourself

"Whether you watched you could otherwise you discovered you cannot, you're proper."

Belief in yourself and your talents is one of the fundamental secrets and strategies of success. Take each other have a take a look at your list of destiny accomplishments this 12 months. Do you in truth consider you can do it?

How To Stick to New Year's Resolutions

Of route, really because of the reality you've were given a strong choice doesn't mean which you're mechanically going to achieve success. As with many changes in existence, it takes effort and time to appearance the outcomes. In what manner, then, are you able to hold your New Year's resolutions?

When it includes keeping your goals, there are a few topics to keep in thoughts. Here are some easy wins:

Remain tenacious. While it could appear apparent, staying strength is vital to moving in advance in any employer. Missing a day or failing to fulfill a milestone doesn't mean that you've failed; it just method you need to try once more tomorrow. You need to hold stimulated.

Be consistent. Similarly, locating a normal to comply with assist you to persist. Fitting in ordinary time on your time desk to paintings towards your purpose manner that it becomes a dependancy, and you may take slow steps.

Learn as you pass. You might also moreover find out that your initial choice isn't pretty proper. It might be too clean, too difficult, or no longer realistic collectively with your modern-day scenario. It's proper to take those commands to coronary coronary heart and modify your desires consequently.

Inform others. You can also additionally hold your resolutions extra accountable with the aid of sharing your aspirations with others.

You may also furthermore allow those closest to you comprehend which you're working toward nice dreams even as no longer having to provide specifics. Then, in case you want assist, they'll offer it.

Guidelines for Effective New Year's Resolutions

This guiding precept for the latest 12 months's resolutions will assist you get off to a a hit begin.

First Rule: Stick to Your Decision

A strong will to trade is the first step in the route of a achievement resolutions. In order to succeed, you have to agree with to your ability to complete the duties accessible. Thus, as you set up them, endure the following in mind:

Make sure your resolutions are optimistic and ones you actually need to meet.

Tell anybody approximately your solve, and they'll assist in keeping you responsible.

Create a ritual to provoke your determination; this may assist it appear extra "actual" and vast to you.

Don't wait till the ultimate minute to select your selection.

Give your targets a few idea. You run the danger of ignoring the larger image and clearly responding to your immediate surroundings if you do now not.

Is this my idea or a person else's? These are a few questions you need to ask yourself to look whether you may take delivery of duty to your cause.

Does this clear up provide me a experience of cause and electricity?

Is this remedy consistent with my prolonged-term goals and ideals, amongst unique factors of my lifestyles?

Recall that wearing out your goal does no longer have to take the complete 12 months.

Advice:

One powerful technique for encouraging you to live with your goals or aspirations is visualization. Consider what it might be need to reach your objective. In what manner are you feeling? How are you? How do unique humans see you?

By seeing yourself inside the feature you need, you can growth your pressure and self notion in your functionality to achieve success. For in addition data, see our internet web page on visualization.

Rule 2: Maintain Realism

Motivation is vital for carrying out dreams. But if you hold your self too excessive, you run the risk of failing.

Be very cautious not to make the identical selection as you probably did the preceding 12 months. If it did no longer artwork lower back then, you want to make sure that there can be a solid foundation for your perception that this yr will carry it about. What has altered?

Instead of aiming too excessive, motive down. Strive for a tough goal that you have a first rate opportunity of attaining.

Aim no large than you could chew. You have to no longer make multiple or resolutions. If you do greater, you'll be dividing your hobby and attempt.

Rule three Put It in Writing

Make a written resolution. It's an clean, however powerful, way to convey your vision to lifestyles. When we take the time to accomplish this, there can be some problem interior us that reacts with greater fervor and determination. Think about putting it down on index playing playing cards and placing it in a seen region. Like in your fridge, table, or pockets, as an example.

Rule four: Create a Schedule

Don't pass this step; it's miles certainly vital!

Start through placing your self inside the favored state of affairs.

After that, trace your path decrease returned for your current area.

Jot down each milestone that needs to be met in among.

Make a plan for undertaking every of those goals. Every step need to be understood, and you must prepare for the following waft.

Rule five: Show Flexibility

Not every state of affairs will unfold exactly as you had expected. The smallest little obstacle could probably derail you, specially in case your method is overly strict. Thus, keep your adaptability and versatility via way of doing the subsequent:

Try to foresee some of the problems you can encounter. As you mentally get prepared for the others, make a backup plan for those which have the most important chance of failing.

Acknowledge the possibility that your solve might also additionally evolve over the years.

That's truth, now not failure. Make a few issue critical changes to the intention that permits you to maintain pursuing it.

It's now not a hard-and-speedy rule that wishes resolutions be made in January. Wait till March; if your state of affairs dictates, that is probably most first rate.

Rule 6: Make Notes

If you have got had been given a number of different commitments, duties, and obligations, it can be tough to stay centered to your technique. To preserve your clear up, create a established reminder system. To do this, keep the subsequent topics in mind:

Make your written dreams to be had. Place reminders in your calendar, to your briefcase, inside the automobile, at paintings, at home, and so forth.

Verify that your to-do listing includes the scheduled duties.

Set your laptop calendar to remind you of the obligations you need to do in case you need to advantage your targets.

Rule 7: Monitor Development

It is vital so that you can apprehend while each milestone is reached because the pride you get from little victories will encourage you to hold going.

Keep a diary and constantly document your upgrades in it.

Write down the moments while you have got been very satisfied collectively with your paintings.

Keep a mag of your low elements and suicidal thoughts.

Regularly assessment your entries to gain statistics out of your studies.

Talk about your improvement with cherished ones, buddies, or coworkers.

Rule eight: Reward Yourself

Sometimes a tiny present or reward is the exceptional manner to provide a person who's already very devoted a lift!

While developing your method, list some dreams which you want to benefit and deal with yourself to when they may be. Spread them apart, however, to ensure that the prizes live unique and tough to get.

Crucial Elements

Make or wreck your New Year's resolutions. You get to make the selection. You can also need to determine not to set resolutions ever once more within the event that they hurt. Decide now to make it interesting!

Focusing on something you are ready to absolutely devote your self to and that you in truth desire is the first step. If you have a take a look at via in this, you'll have a awesome foundation for fulfillment and motivation!

Use those 8 hints to ensure that your New Year's resolutions are as a fulfillment as you endorse them to be.

What Are the Best New Year's Resolutions?

Finding the 'best' selection is, of path, a totally subjective device. It is feasible that what works for you can now not work for others, and vice versa. A useful region to begin is thru identifying what fulfillment technique to you.

As we'll see, there are various matters you could do to make your New Year's resolutions as useful as feasible. To set effective goals, you want to:

Be particular

Set measurable and feasible milestones.

Make them relevant for your existence.

Give organization timescales to reap them.

Essentially, you need to define exactly what you want to advantage and even as you want to collect it, ensuring that you could degree the final effects.

Now, permit's look at some of the maximum well-known' resolutions regularly said. These are taken from severa assets and are in no way a completely accurate degree:

Exercise more

Lose weight

Get organised

Learn a ultra-current expertise.

Eat greater healthy

Save cash

Get a brand new hobby.

Read extra

The lists go on on this style. Can you inform why such masses of people fail?

Many of those aren't precise, measurable, or have time frames associated with them. This makes it difficult to get inside the path of them in any big way.

Chapter 10: Resolution Ideas For 2024

Now which you understand a manner to make resolutions which you as a minimum have the opportunity of sticking to, you can want a few mind for targets we've compiled a listing of a few initial examples of New Year's resolution mind below:

Learn to have a conversation in each exceptional language thru August through operating in the direction of for x hours in line with week.

Start with the beneficial resource of training for as a minimum x hours each month.

By the give up of March, end an internet route to analyze the basics of writing Python code.

Cook one nutritious meal every week for the duration of the spring to decorate your food plan.

Read at the least one ebook a month thru way of committing to examine for half-hour every night earlier than mattress.

Save x quantity each month by way of the usage of using setting up a standing order into a separate economic institution account on the day you gets a fee.

Work to your profession talents and study for a new undertaking in a place you're inquisitive about in the next six months.

You also can regulate the ones examples to fit your desires and manner of existence, or you could use them as idea for something sincerely your very personal. The vital thing is which you're committing to a clean motion inner a selected time frame, with a framework for a manner you're going to advantage it.

Boost Your Goals for The New Year

Before you even start to set up commitments for the New Year, people regularly take two ordinary diversions. Before considering what they absolutely need to perform, they do not forget what is right to do. Second, they consciousness on what they want to give up on as opposed to what they need to perform.

Any exchange calls for a honest preference for your element to be effective. Make a choice that you're not genuinely dedicated to till you make the effort to remember what it is that you truly choice.

Since setting dreams for the cutting-edge twelve months is that this sort of famous custom, they will have great have an impact on. Everybody is conscious that everybody else is organizing. And what a outstanding network for mutual help that may provide!

What may also separate success from failure is that this outside force and encouragement from your self and your desire to gain.

Ideas for New Year's Resolutions and How to Achieve Them

Many people are reflecting on their lives and reassessing a number of their alternatives now that the today's 365 days has arrived. For dad and mom who've no longer commenced out making the modifications they promised to start subsequent week, next month, or possibly at the same time as iciness arrives, the New Year's resolutions offer the right hazard.

As maximum human beings do not study via on their resolutions, now may be it slow to sit down and increase a listing of the number one lifestyle changes you want to make. We've selected to provide you a touch help because of the truth, let's face it, you'll need it.

Self-Improvements for a Better You for the New Year

Here's a fixed of motivational New Year's dreams, alongside side some steerage:

1. Get-in Form

Over one-0.33 of the populace desires to shed pounds, it simply is the pinnacle solve amongst Americans, along thing "workout extra" and "stay wholesome and wholesome." Starting a fitness and nutrients software application isn't always too difficult; the mission is choosing a exceptional one as a way to provide regular results and be manageable over time.

Eat better: Make a healthy food plan adjustment. Consume loads of end end result, greens, and excessive-fiber food.

Become extra lively via signing up for a gymnasium. Try to consist of exercise into your normal exercises, even in case you're too busy. For instance, at artwork, use the steps rather than the elevator.

2. Consume a Healthier Diet

Usually, that is a continuation of the previous selection. A better diet regime can be quite hard to adopt at the identical time as inexpensive junk food is all round us. However, you may grade by grade shape healthful ingesting conduct if you installation a sincere quantity of try and follow a few clean suggestions. Try those nutritious food, emerge as privy to your nutrients, and discover ways to regulate your emotional eating.

Begin by using the use of:

Minimize junk meals intake: Lower the quantity of junk meals you eat. Remove them genuinely out of your food regimen if at all feasible.

Replace processed food with sparkling ones. Preservatives and excessive salt concentrations are common in processed meals. Make a few glowing soup and replace that could of soup.

3. Give Up Postponing

The urge to unwind and do a little thing thrilling instead of artwork tough is the principle impediment that prevents the bulk of people from achieving their goals. It takes an entire lot of attempt to break the terrible addiction of procrastination due to the fact when you get into it, it's far difficult to get out of it.

Although there are some of useful strategies available to help you stop procrastinating, the exceptional advice is to divide the undertaking into smaller steps: When we have got an excessive amount of paintings earlier human beings, we will be predisposed to place it off. Divide the activity into feasible chunks and assign due dates to every chunk.

4. Boost Your Focus

For masses of years, human beings had been attempting to find strategies to boom their capability to pay hobby and anticipate in truth. The majority of ancient societies used a combination of natural medicinal drug and intellectual physical video games to collect this motive.

Consider operating closer to meditation. The mind is skilled to pay interest on one problem at a time via meditation. You might also additionally decorate your interest and recognition via using the usage of meditating.

These days, we may additionally moreover improve our mental abilities and boom our interest via the use of everything from programs to meditation practices. If you have a look at thru in this, you'll be capable of manage your temper, select subjects up more brief, and solve problems extra with out problem.

How Well-Sustained Is Your Life?

Use our Time/Life Self-Assessment to determine how balanced your lifestyles is and get a unfastened, tailor-made file.

You'll discover your competencies in time management, unearth untapped potential, and take manipulate of your lifestyles. Try the free assessment.

five. Make New Friends

When we discover ourselves in a rut, we frequently land up spending most of our time at home and miss out on quite a few interesting opportunities to socialise and network. Don't be scared to go out there and make some buddies, because of the fact doing so may also moreover moreover enhance your mental fitness and improve your career.

Although it might be tough for shy people, this is an first-rate preference for the modern 365 days. To begin with, absolutely take delivery of a chum's invitation to go out one nighttime. This is a honestly wonderful first step in gaining information of recent human beings.

Get out of your comfort area and engage in conversation with one or new people you meet on the fitness center or dancing magnificence.

6 Regular Exercise

Some people might not also be overweight, and they will even exercising some instances consistent with week, however they spend maximum of their time sitting down, every at artwork and at home, which can be negative to their health and posture.

If so, all you want to do is determine out a manner to upward thrust up and flow about more all through the day rather than spend it slumped over a computer. If you include friends and family to your interest, it is a lot extra exciting.

Alternatively, you might certainly start transferring. Instead of ordering takeout to be brought to your home, circulate for a stroll or pace your room.

7. Gain Self-Assurance

Being self-assured makes you greater exquisite to others and makes it an awful lot much less complicated to invite people out, voice your mind, and enhance for your profession. Having a healthful dose of self-self warranty can make your existence hundreds happier in elegant.

Having outstanding self-talk, concentrating for your successes, and seeing failure as a analyzing possibility are all a part of developing self notion.

Additionally, grin more. You will experience better on the identical time as you're grinning. You'll enjoy extra certain at the equal time as you're feeling well.

8. Earn Money to Live Better

Even millionaires are normally searching for new strategies to boom their profits, and the not unusual man or woman should without a doubt advantage from having a 2d source of earnings to live a bit extra and not the usage of a hassle. Fortunately, there are hundreds of opportunities available, such as leveraging the net for your advantage, running as a freelancer, or taking up trouble responsibilities.

Think about taking a 2d mission. Look thru the internet for possible aspect gigs and take some time to installation one.

9. Show More Etiquette

A civilized way of life has lengthy located a immoderate cost on having genuine manners. They facilitate interpersonal connections, assist you live out of hassle, and assure that unique human beings think properly of you.

Thus, exercising correct manners, deal with rude human beings as it need to be, and studies the way to say no without offending a person.

Please, excuse me, sorry, thank you, and pardon me more regularly are the 5 key terms.

10. Lessen Tension

This is sincerely considered one among many wonderful New Year's goals, as strain is one of the principal killers and may have a devastating impact for your relationships and fitness. Although it's far an inevitable byproduct of our busy present day lives, it could be effectively controlled with using sensible and smooth pressure-bargain techniques: How Not to Stress: 10 Strategies for Managing Stress

Plan some "me time" as well so you may additionally additionally unwind and rejuvenate. It may be for some hours every day, or it might be an entire day off.

eleven. Discover How to Be Happy

It is possible to remain miserable even when you have superb health, a strong income, and manipulate your stress. Learning to realize the little pleasures in existence and to maintain your spirits up inside the face of adversity calls for staying energy and time.

Expressing thankfulness is a effective tool for growing satisfaction. To resource in keeping your interest on lifestyles's high exceptional factors, don't forget preserving a gratitude diary. Jot down three subjects for that you are grateful at the cease of every day.

12. Getting Adequate Sleep

Getting ok sleep at night time may be tough with all of the devices which have flashing lights and blaring warnings, which consist of laptops, cell phones, tablets, large TVs, and certainly one of a kind electronics.

Considering your particular sleep chronotype, you need to gather sufficient sleep. Before going to mattress, located your devices away for as a minimum an hour. It is probably a wonderful deal a whole lot less difficult to fall asleep if you allow your thoughts transition into middle of the night mode.

Establish a middle of the night everyday as nicely. Set and preserve a normal bedtime. Every day, try and visit bed and awaken on the identical time.

thirteen. Give Up Smoking Cigarettes

Smoking is a terrible addiction that many people warfare to break because it now not pleasant places your health at danger but also can drain your monetary business enterprise account. Just be geared up to dedicate a huge quantity of energy of will to absolutely quitting smoking.

Addiction healing may be very tough. Seek behavioral remedy, come to be concerned in a assist organisation, or rely upon your own family.

14. Reduce Your TV Watching

The regular American watches TV for approximately eight hours a day—greater than they do for cooking and most probably for slumbering [3]! That is time that would were higher used for studying, growing, or being bodily lively. You turns into privy to how prolonged and effective a day also can really be if you are able to reduce your TV searching time.

15. Continue Reading

Books are a first-rate manner to look at a outstanding deal approximately a large type of topics and also are appropriate intellectual sports activities sports. Finding your preferred sort of e-book, making time for studying (although it is simplest for 10 to 15 minutes a day), and making the dependancy of analyzing are the first-class subjects desired to finish 20 or more books in a three hundred and sixty five days.

sixteen. Locate a Special Someone

Everyone desires someone to speak to, hug at night time time, and confide our darkest secrets and strategies to, but it takes a few trial and mistakes to discover the right person.

Before we are able to find out the character with whom we click on on the maximum, we want to go out and meet a number of possible pals.

Use the ones tips to ask a person out and characteristic a memorable and precise first date to get inspired to your route to locating love.

17. Enjoy Better Sexual Relations

A huge stage of closeness is critical in every a success courting, and having intercourse might also moreover honestly improve our bodily and emotional well-being [4]. Making it a laugh and gratifying is the intention, and that is some detail that can be completed with exercise and exercise.

18. Maintain More Orders

It allows to put off the clutter, smooth your property, and lead a tidier and extra organized life. There are masses of slobs accessible who can not definitely hold their matters looked after, and a crowded table or chaotic domestic can appreciably have an impact for your productivity or even your temper.

19. Discover How to Wear Style

Your look conveys loads about you, and dressing well may also additionally assist you seem sturdy and confident, as a manner to can help you accumulate a procedure, enhance for your career, and enchantment to the attention of attractive human beings. Regardless of gender, dress to stand out in a crowd with the aid of manner of sporting some thing that makes you revel in accurate about yourself.

20. Give Important People More Time

We certainly do no longer have sufficient time on this lifestyles to spend it on poisonous, deceitful, and dishonest people. The finest technique to stay satisfied and characteristic a fulfilling existence is to put our interest on the people who care deeply about us.

21. Reduce Your Alcohol Consumption

Although ingesting one or servings [5] of any shape of alcoholic beverage consistent with day is flawlessly strong and healthy, few individuals can really declare a wonderful way to paste to this recommendation. Although there are numerous blessings to controlling your ingesting, it is able to be a difficult enterprise enterprise.

Begin slowly. If you regularly have glasses of wine after paintings, attempt lowering that proper down to honestly one for a month.

After that, keep in mind restricting your consumption to 1 or two glasses every week.

22. Eliminate Debt

If debt is retaining you once more in lifestyles, it's far truely no longer viable to move in advance. Although accomplishing economic independence is a tough journey, it's miles without a doubt practicable with a few education and electricity of mind. Examine those strategies to debt repayment. It will revel in so superb which you can not accept as actual with it.

23. Saving Money

It's time to start placing coins apart after your debt is under control. A wet-day reserve and some spare coins that may be used for distant places trips, domestic protection, or new car purchases are smooth options. Try these powerful cash-saving techniques.

24.   Learn a New Language

Acquiring skills in a cutting-edge language will now not pleasant beautify your capacity to speak, but it's going to moreover upload price in your CV and even purpose career opportunities. There are many internet web sites to be had nowadays that assist you to studies a language at no cost.

25. Volunteer More and Donate to Charities

Giving your time and effort to those in need is not excellent a type deed and one of the in reality worthwhile New Year's desires, but it's also a risk to network, select up new competencies, and enhance your CV. Here's the way to suit volunteering into your traumatic time desk.

25. Develop Useful Skills or Enjoyable Interests

It might not assist to absolutely sit down round all day. It is an entire lot maximum famous to make efficient use of your Leisure time, studies new talents, and enjoy yourself whilst doing so. Later on, you may be satisfied which you took this motion. Whether you are into athletics or conversation competencies, find out the way to pick out up new skills and interests rapid.

26. Give Up Resentment

While it may take masses to conquer problem and tough times, moping about ineffectively solves not anything. You will wonderful lose a chum or life accomplice and live depressed and resentful in case you get proper right into a heated argument with a person and turn out to be disappointed over a touch conflict of phrases. Dealing with difficulties that ought to be left inside the beyond is lots better even as accomplished through forgiveness.

27. Get a Pet.

Many people who love animals and can be superb domestic dog proprietors overthink subjects, at the same time as others clearly exit and adopt a puppy with out understanding the responsibility that includes it. Make terrific you're prepared and select a puppy that enhances your manner of life and residing state of affairs.

28. Organize Yourself Better

No rely how a bargain loose time you have, if you cannot manage it nicely, you could first-class wind up dropping maximum of the day circling round. Thus, on the top of your listing of New Year's dreams must be organisation. Organizing your self will unfastened up greater time, and subjects will begin to fall into region. Develop the dependancy, use gadget and programs for help, and experience your newly determined free time.

29. Take More Trips

Before you ponder traveling the sector, you can want to get your cash so as, gather the crucial equipment, and established some effort and time. However, there are strategies to look remote locations and revel in diverse cultures even on a restricted budget.

To fulfill your wanderlust, watch a few documentaries, move on a vacation, or change letters with a pen buddy remote places.

30. Acquire Cooking Skills

One of the maximum crucial capabilities that any individual want to have is cooking. It lets you consume the delicacies you want precisely the way you need it, shop money, and wow dates with romantic dinners loved through candlelight.

Maintaining your fitness must be your first issue, however an entire lot of people do not see the clinical medical health practitioner as frequently as they need to due to the truth they appear frightened of them, from time to time ready till their contamination has end up an lousy lot worse. Regardless of strategies well you may enjoy proper now, normal examinations are vital.

31. Take a New Look at Yourself

One of your smart New Year's desires need to be to make a few massive modifications in your existence in case you discover that no matter what you do, you're in no way in truth satisfied. You can also additionally additionally have a whole new outlook on life and bypass places you couldn't have idea were feasible through reinventing your self.

32. Quit Being Late

Being punctual is pretty valued in our manner of life; therefore, making this your New Year's intention is a exceptional concept. Learn the behaviors of punctual humans to stay on time. Being on time is a image of a real professional, a honest friend, and a loving associate.

33. Become More Independent

We were noticeably spoiled thru era, a pretty actual authorities, and businesses that offer less pricey, ready-to-consume food and a plethora of beneficial devices. As a stop end result, we regularly gain adulthood with out owning the crucial talents to be independent and self-reliant. Try dealing with the hassle on your own the subsequent time in place of speeding to the nearest friend or family member.

34. Make a Career Out of Your Interest

We may additionally all be masses happier and function a extra balanced society if we must all determine out the manner to integrate amusement with artwork and earn a dwelling doing what we adore. While it is able to now not commonly be possible, there are instances wherein taking over a extremely-current hobby might probable motive a a achievement profession.

35. Let Go of Your Past

Even if it hurts masses, it could be most exceptional to have loved and misplaced than to have in no way cherished. Although mending a shattered coronary coronary heart is a sluggish technique, self-care is step one in surviving this attempting period with minimal struggling.

36. Develop Emotional Self-Control

While unchecked rage may additionally bring about many issues, controlling your emotions is an incredible New Year's choice considering emotions like pleasure and envy can be dangerous in any scenario. Developing emotional self-discipline permits you to stay composed and make extra logical choices, even in the face of extreme emotional conflict.

37. Be More Responsible

The functionality to keep in mind options earlier than performing is a crucial element of developing right right into a responsible man or woman. Just because it's essential to defend your circle of relatives and assist in imparting for them, it is also essential to without a doubt be given obligation for one's actions and refrain from putting the blame some area else.

38. Expand Your Knowledge of Culture, Music, And Art

Having a well-rounded training is the fantastic way to aggregate in at the identical time as interacting with a severa kind of human beings from various backgrounds. Although many people discover it hard to recognize, topics like records, art work, music, and culture can also truly be as an alternative simple if you take the time to take a look at them.

39. Minimize Your Social MediaTime

While some people might not spend a number of time looking TV or playing video video video games, social media has become a number one dependancy for humans in many exclusive demographic businesses. Maintaining relationships with buddies and family is OK, but in case you discover yourself the use of social media for additonal than an hour a day, it's time to make a exchange and put this on your list of profitable New Year's dreams.

40. Acquire Self-Defense Skills

It's vital to own the competencies critical to guard every your non-public protection and the protection of the humans you care about. But it's miles no longer best approximately palm actions and groin kicks. It is vital that you purchased expertise approximately proper conduct, each for yourself and others.

41. Embrace Romanticism More

In partnerships that final longer and are greater vital, romance regularly finally ends up death first, but it doesn't must. The romance can also very last for many years if you high-quality plan date evenings and spend time collectively. Even in case you're now not the romantic kind, it'll nonetheless be interesting.

40. Recall Vital Dates

When it involves romance and maintaining the joy of a devoted relationship, you do now not want to typically forget about milestones like anniversaries and birthdays. You might not ever forget approximately another date yet again for the cause that there are a ton of reminiscence techniques which may be easy to research.

forty three. Increase Your Social Media Presence

There are advantages to going out and mingling. This is a fantastic New Year's selection to add to your listing while you keep in mind that now not great are you capable of study new subjects, have amusing, and meet new humans, but you may moreover hone your leadership abilities and teamwork capabilities. There are approaches to take part quite actively in a community, even if you are an introvert, very shy, or locate it difficult to talk to others.

forty four. Foster Greater Originality

There are moments while we just lose our creativity because of highbrow exhaustion. This is especially complex if your line of exertions or passion calls if you want to anticipate creatively and unconventionally. Like the whole lot else, there are various techniques to inspire your innovative go with the drift.

forty five.   Use Art to Express Yourself

The majority humans although own a piece creativity, in spite of the truth that some of us are more rational. Making innovative expressions of oneself is a brilliant technique to relax and preserve highbrow clarity. You may also additionally furthermore stay energetic and burn some energy through taking issue in a number of those sports activities. Write, create, and do-it-your self initiatives—do some trouble that releases your spirit.

Chapter 11: Compassion And Self Kindness

Learning from Mistakes

Forgiving your self is a profound and transformative device that includes granting oneself compassion, knowledge, and recognition for beyond mistakes or shortcomings. Initially, it calls for acknowledging the humanity in oneself, statistics that everybody is fallible and vulnerable to making mistakes. This step includes recognizing that selfforgiveness is an critical a part of personal boom and emotional recuperation, allowing humans to transport ahead from the load of selfblame or guilt.

Furthermore, forgiving yourself includes letting skip of selfcondemnation and embracing selfcompassion. It necessitates treating oneself with kindness, empathy, and facts, just like how one might amplify forgiveness to others. This workout includes freeing the cruel judgments or lousy selfspeak related to past actions, fostering a revel in of emotional liberation and internal peace.

Moreover, forgiving yourself encompasses accepting duty at the same time as detaching from immoderate selfblame. It includes acknowledging one's function in past sports without residing on selfcondemnation or defining oneself completely thru beyond mistakes. This step allows humans to observe from critiques at the same time as stopping those errors from defining their selfworth or future actions.

Additionally, forgiving oneself consists of a manner of personal growth and healing. It requires actively working inside the direction of selfdevelopment and the use of beyond critiques as schooling for personal development. This transformative adventure consists of cultivating a mindset of resilience, mastering, and evolving surely from beyond missteps.

The advantages of forgiving your self are massive. Firstly, it contributes to emotional nicelybeing by way of reducing feelings of guilt, disgrace, or selfdoubt. Secondly, it fosters inner peace and a experience of empowerment, allowing people to embrace a greater fine and selfaffirming outlook on lifestyles.

Integrating selfforgiveness into one's life includes willpower to selfreflected photograph, selfcompassion, and private increase. This includes running closer to selfreputation, letting drift of selfcriticism, and actively running in the direction of selfimprovement. By embracing selfforgiveness, people embark on a journey inside the course of selfrecovery, emotional resilience, and a deeper experience of selfcompassion and knowledge.

It's an interior approach that consists of acknowledging previous errors or moves that motive guilt and choosing to allow circulate of the related horrible emotions. It's about displaying selfcompassion and statistics that making mistakes is a phase of being human.

This act of selfforgiveness does not endorse forgetting or condoning previous actions but as an opportunity accepting them as section of your journey. It involves:

1. Acceptance:Acknowledging the past without residing on it excessively, spotting that everybody makes mistakes.

2. Compassion: Being type to yourself and expertise which you are treasured of forgiveness but beyond mistakes or regrets.

three. Letting Go: Releasing the emotional weight tied to past movements, freeing yourself from the burden of guilt or shame.

four. Learning and Growth: Reflecting on beyond testimonies, appreciation the training they offer, and the usage of them as opportunities for private boom and development.

Forgiving your self is a transformative act that approves you to move beforehand with a lighter heart and a more effective outlook on existence. It's approximately granting yourself the identical expertise and forgiveness you'll in all likelihood with out problems extend to others, recognizing your inherent worthiness of selfcompassion.

This internal shift fosters emotional recuperation, promotes selfelegance, and empowers you to include the winning second with large peace and resilience.

Compassion and selfkindness within the context of forgiving your self incorporate cultiating a mindset of perception and empathy within the path of your very nonpublic actions and studies. It's about:

1. SelfCompassion: Treating yourself with the identical kindness and care that you may offer to a chum handling a similar scenario.

2. Understanding Fallibility: Recognizing that making mistakes is a stylish phase of the human enjoy, and these errors do not define your really genuinely really worth.

three. NonJudgment: Avoiding harsh selfgrievance and as an alternative acknowledging your moves with an open and understanding mindset.

4. Acceptance:

Embracing your imperfections and appreciation that selfforgiveness doesn't mean erasing past moves but as an opportunity permitting your self to move earlier.

Cultivating selfcompassion and selfkindness is pivotal internal the adventure of selfforgiveness. It permits you to technique preceding errors with belief and empathy, fostering a extra healthy dating with yourself and merchandising emotional restoration.

Learning from mistakes is a way of introspection and growth that entails deriving insights and facts from previous studies or mistakes. Here's a unique breakdown:

Learning from Mistakes

Growth Mindset

Positive Perspective: Embrace a mindset that views errors as possibilities for reading and personal improvement.

Adopting Curiosity: Approach mistakes with hobby in place of fear, searching out to apprehend what went wrong and why.

Reflection and Analysis

SelfReflection: Take time to copy on the occasions, picks, and moves that brought on the mistake or undesirable outcome.

Identifying Patterns: Look for habitual subjects or behaviors that could have contributed to the error.

Extracting Lessons

Identifying Insights: Find the schooling or records won from the error, appreciation how it is capable to inform destiny selections.

Preventive Measures: Use the insights gained to growth strategies to keep away from similar errors in the destiny.

Embracing Growth

Implementing Changes: Actively look at the instructions decided to make satisfactory adjustments in conduct, mindset, or preferencemaking.

Accepting Imperfection: Embrace the thinking that making mistakes is a herbal segment of increase and development.

Importance of Learning from Mistakes

Personal Development:Extracting instructions from errors fosters private growth, resilience, and flexibility.

Wisdom Accumulation: Each mistake becomes a deliver of expertise, contributing to better choicemaking and hasslefixing competencies.

Learning from mistakes is now not about residing on the error but about gleaning insights that might steer future movements in a extra knowledgeable and first rate course. It's a important detail of growth and improvement, allowing humans to comply and beautify through the years.

Chapter 12: Mindfulness Practices

Journaling and Reflection

Letting move strategies are strategies or practices geared in the path of freeing emotional burdens, including previous guilt or terrible reports, to encompass a greater excessive remarkable and non violent present. Here's a complete breakdown:

Letting Go Techniques

Mindfulness Practices

Present Moment Awareness: Focus at the triumphing 2d barring judgment, allowing thoughts and emotions to bypass without attachment.

Breath Awareness: Engage in conscious respiratory exercising workout routines to anchor yourself in the present day and permit circulate of intrusive thoughts.

Visualization and Imagery

Release Rituals: Visualize liberating bad feelings or beyond reviews through imagining them dissipating or being carried away.

Positive Future Visualization: Imagine a terrific, guiltloose future to shift focal component faraway from past regrets.

Journaling and Reflection

Writing Exercises: Journal about your feelings, thoughts, and reviews, taking into consideration selfmirrored image and a enjoy of emotional release.

Letter Writing: Consider writing a letter to your self or any character else worried within the scenario, expressing your emotions and intentions to allow cross.

Acceptance and Surrender

Acceptance of Emotions: Acknowledge and take transport of your mind barring making an attempt to suppress or manage them.

Surrendering Control: Understand that some topics are beyond your control, and letting bypass includes accepting this reality.

Physical Release Practices

Movement and Exercise: Engaging in physical sports activities can assist release pentup feelings and pressure, promoting a enjoy of letting pass.

Relaxation Techniques: Practices like yoga, meditation, or innovative muscle relaxation can useful resource in liberating tension and emotional luggage.

Importance of Letting Go

Emotional Freedom: Letting pass frees you from the burden of past regrets or guilt, considering emotional restoration and growth.

Living inside the Present: It lets in you to center of hobby at the triumphing 2d, fostering a enjoy of peace and contentment.

Letting flow strategies are bendy and may be customized to move properly with man or woman alternatives and needs. They empower humans to release emotional burdens, fostering emotional nicelybeing and a greater immoderate superb outlook on existence.

Mindfulness practices involve being in reality gift and aware about the currentdayday 2d with out judgment. It's approximately cultivating a kingdom of focused interest on mind, emotions, bodily sensations, or the encompassing surroundings.

Mindfulness Practices

Present Moment Awareness

Focused Attention: Directing interest to the moderndayday second, acknowledging mind and sensations as they rise up.

NonJudgmental Observation: Observing thoughts with out assigning them rate or judgment.

Breath Awareness

Centering Technique: Using the breath as an anchor to preserve center of interest lower once more to the contemporary moment.

Stress Reduction: Engaging in conscious breathing to relieve pressure and promote rest.

Mindful Activities

Everyday Mindfulness: Incorporating mindfulness into every day sports, including aware ingesting, walking, or listening.

Sensory Awareness: Paying interest to senses—sight, sound, taste, touch, and scent—to floor oneself inside the present 2d.

Benefits of Mindfulness

Stress Reduction: Mindfulness practices can decrease stress thru way of selling a enjoy of calm and relaxation.

Enhanced Wellbeing: Regular mindfulness exercise is related to advanced intellectual readability, emotional law, and everyday nicelybeing.

Application in Letting Go

1) Release of Emotions: Mindfulness permits acknowledgment and popularity of emotions, helping of their release.

2) Focus on the Present: By specializing inside the present 2d, it allows humans permit bypass of past regrets or destiny issues.

Mindfulness is a powerful tool inside the exercising of letting pass. By cultivating mindfulness, humans can improve a extended potential to release emotional burdens, sell selfinterest, and embody the triumphing second with higher ease and clarity.

Journaling and contemplated image involve the act of introspection thru writing approximately one's mind, emotions, and research. It's a device for selfdiscovery and emotional processing besides the restrictions of judgment or outside validation.

Journaling and Reflection

1) SelfExpression

Emotional Outlet:Writing serves as a regular residence to particular feelings, allowing for the release of pentup emotions.

Clarity of Thoughts:Putting thoughts on paper helps set up and make clear complex emotions or situations.

2) SelfExploration

Insight Generation:Writing lets in for deeper selfexploration, revealing patterns or connections among mind and behaviors.

Identification of Triggers:Recognizing triggers or elements contributing to great feelings or behaviors via reflected photo.

three) Emotional Processing

Cathartic Effect: Journaling can function a cathartic release, providing a sense of consolation or closure concerning preceding activities.

Emotional Healing: Reflecting on critiques fosters emotional appreciation and aids in the technique of recuperation.

4) Personal Growth

Learning and Development: Documenting reviews permits mastering from errors and appreciation personal boom over time.

Goal Setting and Tracking: Journaling can help set goals, track development, and feature amusing achievements, contributing to personal development.

5) Letting Go

Release of Emotions: Writing approximately previous guilt or regrets permits notably diagnosed and launch related emotions, merchandising the system of letting go with the flow.

Creating Space for Acceptance: Reflecting on beyond memories approves for popularity and understanding, facilitating the letting go with the flow method.

Journaling and mirrored picture provide a powerful capability to find out feelings, benefit insights, and facilitate emotional processing. It allows human beings to navigate through past studies, fostering increase, knowhow, and ultimately, letting skip of emotional burdens.

Gratitude Exercises

Setting PresentCentered

Embracing the triumphing consists of immersing oneself clearly inside the contemporaryday 2d except being preoccupied thru way of the usage of thoughts of the past or troubles approximately the destiny. It's about:

1. Being Fully Present: Engaging wholeheartedly in a few thing interest or state of affairs you're presently experiencing barring distraction or judgment.

2. Appreciating the Now: Recognizing and cherishing the richness and beauty of the winning second, no matter its simplicity.

three. Letting Go of Control: Accepting that some things are beyond your control and embracing the uncertainty of the future with openness and flexibility.

4. Fostering a Positive Mindset: Cultivating optimism and gratitude through focusing at the positives inside the present as an opportunity than dwelling on regrets or worries.

five. Active Engagement: Actively taking thing in relationships, tales, and sports, making an investment your interest and power actually.

Embracing the moderndayday capability consciously selecting to stay lifestyles in the proper right right here and now, locating pleasure and contentment inside the current second, and appreciating the richness of each adventure as it unfolds. It's about liberating your self from the burden of past regrets and future uncertainties, permitting you to locate peace and achievement within the present.

Gratitude sports activities are practices geared closer to cultivating a thoughtsset centered on acknowledging and appreciating the immoderate quality elements of lifestyles. Here's a proper rationalization of those physical games:

Gratitude Exercises

1) Gratitude Journaling

Daily Entries:Write down property you are thankful for, whether or now not huge or small, to mirror at the positives for your existence.

Specificity: Be unique about what you appreciate, detailing why it holds significance for you.

2) Gratitude Reflection

Mindful Moments: Set aside time to mirror on research or people you're thankful for, allowing your self to absolutely immerse in those feelings.

Internal Acknowledgment: Mentally precise gratitude for the ones testimonies or people, acknowledging their have an effect on on your lifestyles.

three) Gratitude Letters or Notes

Expressive Writing:Write a letter or be conscious to any individual you're grateful for, expressing your knowhow and explaining why they are significant to you.

Personal Delivery: Consider turning inside the letter or word in character or certainly to beautify the relationship.

4) Gratitude in Daily Conversations

Expressing Thanks:Integrate expressions of gratitude into each day conversations, acknowledging and appreciating others.

Highlighting Positives: Focus on what goes on properly or what you admire in loads of interactions.

5) Benefits of Gratitude Exercises

Increased Positivity: Practicing gratitude enhances immoderate quality emotions, crucial to an extended conventional outlook on life.

Emotional Wellbeing: It reduces emotions of pressure and negativity, fostering emotional resilience.

6) Integration in Letting Go

Integration in letting pass includes a multilayered approach of merging insights from acknowledging past guilt with the exercise of freeing oneself from its emotional grip. In the primary segment, it encompasses the information won from recognizing past actions or selections that delivered approximately emotions of regret or regret. This knowhow serves as a foundational issue, highlighting the feelings' origins and their impact on present mind and behaviors.

Moving earlier, integration in letting pass involves the assimilation of those insights into the journey of emotional launch. This segment recognizes that the popularity of past movements is critical to transferring beyond their emotional weight. It turns on human beings to confront those feelings with compassion and data, fostering selfreputation and setting out the recovery method. This reputation paperwork the bridge among acknowledging past guilt and releasing oneself from its lingering effects.

The next section includes leveraging the assimilated insights to catalyze a transformative shift in thoughtsset. This shift reframes past errors as opportunities for increase and studying, fostering a forwardsearching and amazing attitude. It involves reframing the narrative surrounding beyond movements, permitting people to attract commands from the ones critiques with out being tethered to their emotional luggage. This altered mindset will become the cornerstone for a liberated mindset, developing space for private growth and resilience.

Finally, integration in letting skip culminates within the energetic software application of those covered insights in the present second. It involves consciously assignment mindfulness practices, leveraging the assimilated understanding to honestly encompass the prevailing with readability, gratitude, and a renewed experience of reason. This phase marks the fruits of the combination machine, wherein the amalgamation of beyond acknowledgments ends in a liberated usa, allowing individuals to navigate life's demanding situations with a newfound feel of emotional freedom and wellbeing.

Gratitude bodily sports serve as powerful tool in shifting one's recognition from terrible elements to the abundance of positives in life. They promote emotional nicelybeing, foster a exquisite mindset, and make a contribution substantially to the tool of letting cross and embracing the winning 2nd.

Setting presenttargeted goals consists of organising desires which is probably centered at the modernday 2nd and align together together with your right now priorities and values. Here's a particular rationalization:

7) Setting PresentCentered Goals

Clarity of Purpose

Identification of Priorities:Assess what topics most to you inside the present 2nd, considering your values and aspirations.

Realistic Focus: Set goals which can be feasible inside the modern context and timebody.

Specificity and Intent

Clear Definition: Define your goals with precision, outlining unique moves or steps vital to acquire them.

Purposeful Alignment: Ensure your goals align together along with your current conditions and make a contribution in your preferred properlybeing.

ActionOriented Approach

Immediate Action Steps: Break down huge dreams into ability responsibilities that may be acted upon inside the gift.

Focus on the Now: Frame goals that may be pursued and accomplished in the gift second or near destiny.

Flexibility and Adaptability

Openness to Change:Embrace flexibility in purposeputting, adjusting them as your present times evolve.

Adaptation to Realities:Modify desires to flow nicely with changing wishes, closing privy to the prevailing surroundings.

Benefits of PresentCentered Goals

Increased Motivation: Goals set inside the present 2d deliver a revel in of immediacy and motivation for movement.

Enhanced Focus: By focusing on cuttingedge goals, it reduces distraction and will increase popularity on what needs to be finished now.

Setting gifttargeted desires entails aligning aspirations with present day occasions, emphasizing right now movement, and adapting to the evolving present. These goals function guides for massive movements and facilitate a feel of purpose and course inside the contemporary 2nd.

Chapter 13: Building A Positive Mindset

Affirmations and Positive Self Talk

Surrounding Yourself with Positivity

Building a pleasing mindset consists of cultivating a mental thoughtsset that specializes in optimism, resilience, and positive wondering. Here's a clearly one in all a type rationalization:

1) Building a Positive Mindset

Optimistic Outlook

Positive Interpretation:Reframe annoying situations or setbacks as opportunities for increase in choice to insurmountable limitations.

Focus on Solutions: Direct interest in the direction of finding answers and possibilities in preference to living on issues.

2) Gratitude and Appreciation

Acknowledging Positives: Cultivate gratitude by means of the use of the use of frequently acknowledging and appreciating the right topics on your life.

Mindful Appreciation: Pay hobby to small moments of joy or kindness, fostering a enjoy of gratitude.

3) SelfCompassion and SelfTalk

Kindness to Self: Practice selfcompassion thru treating yourself with the same kindness you may offer a pal in difficult instances.

Positive SelfTalk: Monitor and exchange horrible selfcommunicate with placing beforehand and supportive messages.

4) Resilience and Adaptability

Acceptance of Change: Embrace alternate as a herbal section of life, adapting and reading from new situations.

Resilience Building: Develop resilience with the aid of the use of the usage of bouncing once more from adversity and setbacks, seeing them as studying opportunities.

five) Mindfulness and Present Focus

Present Moment Awareness: Engage in mindfulness practices to center your self within the gift 2d, decreasing worry about the beyond or destiny.

Living in the Now: Focus on the existing 2nd, coming across pleasure and contentment within the proper right proper right here and now.

Benefits of a Positive Mindset

Enhanced Mental Health:Promotes emotional wellbeing with the aid of using decreasing strain, anxiety, and horrible emotions.

Improved ProblemSolving:Facilitates clearer questioning and revolutionary hasslesolving abilties.

Integration in Letting Go

Release of Negative Emotions: Building a high satisfactory mindset allows in letting pass of beyond regrets or guilt with the useful useful resource of fostering a more superb outlook.

Mindset Shift: Embracing positivity shifts the point of interest from living on the past to embracing the present with a more hopeful mindset.

Building a excessive brilliant mindset entails intentional exercising and a determination to cultivating fantastic thoughts and attitudes. It's a powerful tool for emotional wellbeing, resilience, and a more fun outlook on lifestyles.

Affirmations and top notch selftalk are techniques that consist of consciously the usage of encouraging and supportive language to uplift and inspire oneself. They middle of hobby on fostering a extra wonderful and opt mistic inner talk.

Affirmations and Positive SelfTalk

Affirmations and top notch selfcommunicate are effective gear that shape thoughts, emotions, and beliefs. The workout consists of using encouraging, declaring statements or inner dialogues to cultivate a top notch mindset and bolster vanity. Initially, affirmations serve as concise, extremely good statements frequently repeated to oneself. These statements are deliberately crafted to counter horrible thoughts, beliefs, or selfperceptions, nurturing a greater tremendous internal communicate. They act as beacons of positivity, influencing one's subconscious mind to enhance useful thoughts and attitudes.

Positive selfcommunicate, alternatively, extends beyond set affirmations to encompass an ongoing, supportive inner talk. This talk consists of consciously addressing oneself with kindness, encouragement, and optimism. It consists of converting terrible selftalk with nurturing, empowering language, fostering a feel of selfcompassion and selfnotion. It's a chronic method in which humans actively show their internal mind, redirecting negativity toward positive and affirmative selftalk.

The blessings of affirmations and best selfcommunicate are a protracted manneraccomplishing. Firstly, they considerably effect one's highbrow and emotional wellbeing with the aid of countering horrific ideals or emotions. Affirmations and high amazing selfcommunicate act as emotional regulators, decreasing pressure, anxiety, and fostering a greater firstrate outlook on existence. Moreover, they contribute to improving selfself notion, arrogance, and resilience by using reinforcing exquisite ideals and selfperceptions.

Integration of affirmations and first rate selfcommunicate into each day life includes everyday workout and mindfulness. This includes the conscious adoption of affirmations in diverse bureaucracy – written, spoken, or even visualized – to reaffirm nice ideals frequently. Similarly, cultivating excellent selftalk requires vigilance in monitoring and redirecting terrible internal dialogues towards more excessive fine and empowering mind. The integration manner involves incorporating those practices into every day physical video games, fostering a mindset shift inside the course of more selfcompassion, selfnotion, and emotional resilience.

In essence, affirmations and wonderful selfcommunicate feature transformative system, influencing thoughts, feelings, and in the long run conduct. They empower human beings to domesticate a greater splendid and nurturing courting with themselves, primary to stronger emotional properlybeing, selfself perception, and a greater powerful outlook on existence's annoying conditions.

Affirmations and satisfactory selfcommunicate function equipment for building a more supportive and inspiring inner speak, vending selfself warranty, and facilitating a mindset shift towards positivity and selfempowerment.

Surrounding your self with positivity involves consciously choosing environments, relationships, and impacts that promote a revel in of optimism, encouragement, and assist to your lifestyles.

www.ingramcontent.com/pod-product-compliance
Lightning Source LLC
Chambersburg PA
CBHW071444080526
44587CB00014B/1989